THE GENTRY 1540–1640

By H. R. TREVOR-ROPER

I

ERHAPS no man has stimulated the study of English history in the
sixteenth century more effectively than Prof. Tawney: the century
from 1540 to 1640, the century which separates the Dissolution of
the Monasteries from the Great Rebellion, may almost be defined, thanks
to his radical reinterpretation of it, as 'Tawney's century'. All historians·
who have since studied that period are inevitably, even if unconsciously,
affected by his reinterpretation: they can no more think of it now in pre-
Tawney terms than sociologists can think of society in pre-Marxist terms.
Nevertheless history, like sociology, is an empirical science, and the
imaginative work of intellectual pioneers must often be modified by the
more pedestrian research which they have themselves inspired. In particular I believe that Prof. Tawney's interpretation is evidentially weak in
two important respects which, advanced by him as a hypothesis, are now
in danger of becoming an orthodoxy. I refer to his hypothesis of 'the rise
of the gentry', based, as he suggests, on new agricultural techniques, and
his parallel hypothesis of the contemporaneous decline of the aristocracy,
caused, as he maintains, by a combination of economic conservatism with
fashionable extravagance. I believe both these hypotheses to be not indeed
incorrect, but wrongly formulated, and I believe that the faulty formulation of them seriously affects our understanding of political as well as of
economic history. In a previous article[1] I have already given my reasons
for rejecting the extremist theory that the Elizabethan aristocracy were on
the verge of bankruptcy, and in the course of that article I have briefly
suggested that the parallel theory of the 'rise of the gentry' is also in some
respects questionable. This suggestion has since—such is the force of
orthodoxy—been summarily dismissed as a 'paradox'. I therefore intend,
in this essay, to follow up my suggestion in detail. I believe it will appear,
first, that the distinction between aristocracy and gentry, as if they were
separate social classes, is an arbitrary distinction; and, secondly, that even
if such a distinction be allowed, the conclusion that 'the aristocracy' was
being replaced by 'the gentry' in the manner suggested is not only un-
supported by such evidence as has been adduced, but is positively repug-
nant to it. After discussing these questions, I shall advance a different
interpretation of the social changes of the period, which I believe to be

---

[1] 'The Elizabethan Aristocracy, An Anatomy Anatomized.' *Econ. Hist. Rev.*
(1951) 2nd ser. III. My views are not modified by Mr Stone's rejoinder, 'The
Elizabethan Aristocracy, A Restatement' (*Econ. Hist. Rev.* (1952) 2nd ser. IV)
in which he anyway seldom quotes me correctly. See also below p. 33, note 1.

better supported by the evidence and alone compatible with the political history which accompanied and illustrated them.

It will be most convenient to begin with a brief summary of Prof. Tawney's thesis. This is clearly presented in three now famous essays: in his introduction to Thomas Wilson's *Discourse on Usury* (1925), in which he incidentally assembled some of the literary evidence for the decline of the aristocracy; in his article on the 'Rise of the Gentry' (*Econ. Hist. Rev.* xi, 1941), in which he described at length both these alleged processes; and in his Raleigh Lecture, 'Harrington's Interpretation of his Age' (1941), in which he recognized in James Harrington, the author of *Oceana*, a previous observer of the same supposed social phenomenon. These three works are complementary, and the picture which they paint of 'Tawney's England' is consistent and similar. They portray an age in which 'the gentry' are acquiring wealth, land, education, confidence and power not merely as their share in the general enrichment of society, but disproportionately, in isolation, at the expense of all the other landed classes in that society, which were consequently in decay. The aristocracy, through 'personal extravagance and political ineptitude', were sinking into 'ruin'; the yeomanry were in 'decline'; only the gentry 'steadily gathered into their hands estates slipping from the grasp of peasant, nobility, church and Crown alike'. The result was a shift in 'the centre of social gravity', 'a new equilibrium', which Prof. Tawney brilliantly lights up with sudden luminous flickers of suggestive metaphor and historical intuition.

How did this 'new equilibrium' arise? To this question Prof. Tawney has a firm answer. The English peerage and the English gentry, he explains, differed, in the sixteenth century, not merely quantitatively, in the acreage of their estates, but also qualitatively, in their methods of managing them. In the sixteenth century there was an agrarian crisis; the crisis put a premium on businesslike methods; and since these businesslike methods were a monopoly of the gentry, who alone understood 'the business side of land-management', aristocratic economy meant estate-management at a loss, gentry economy meant estate-management at a profit. Thus by a necessary consequence of this simple difference, the peerage could hardly fail to founder or the gentry to prosper. This interesting distinction between unbusinesslike aristocratic economy and businesslike gentry economy is illustrated by Prof. Tawney at some length and in some detail. The aristocracy, he explains, were committed to heavy overheads and obsolete methods: they therefore found their expenses steadily rising and 'their real incomes not less steadily diminishing'; on the other hand, the gentry, 'in process of conversion to up-to-date methods of land-management', found their income automatically rising. Thus the crisis of the time 'was felt more acutely, and surmounted with greater difficulty, by the heirs of ancient wealth...than by men of humbler position or more recent eminence', and the advantages were all inevitably on the side not of the peer who only knew the difficulties of the time, but of 'the enterprising country gentleman'.

Thus Prof. Tawney's thesis consists of two major hypotheses. First there is the phenomenon which he states as a fact—the 'new equilibrium' caused by the decline of the aristocracy and the rise of the gentry; secondly, there is the explanation of this phenomenon which in turn is another statement of fact, viz. that the gentry understood and practised land-management as the aristocracy did not. The explanation, if substantiated, is obviously an adequate explanation of the phenomenon, if that can be substantiated. The question is, can they be substantiated? What is the evidence for these two statements of fact, first, that the aristocracy were being replaced by the gentry; secondly, that the gentry improved their estates while the aristocracy did not?

For this double phenomenon Prof. Tawney adduces two groups of evidence. First there is contemporary literary evidence (consisting of protestations of poverty by the peers themselves and observations thereon by competent judges); secondly, there are modern statistics. It must be admitted that none of this evidence is very strong, and Prof. Tawney himself handles it with great diffidence. Thus, in 'The Rise of the Gentry', having begun with a positive statement—'The facts were plain enough'—he is content to describe the contemporary literary observations as 'a stream of comment' upon these apparently incontestable facts. Later in the same essay, with equal modesty, he describes the modern statistics as 'some casual scraps of statistical evidence' which, if the contemporary literary observers had 'shared the modern taste for figures', would have provided support for their observations. It will be noted that the allegedly plain facts are deduced neither from the statistics nor from the observations, both of which are tentatively admitted only as possible corroborations of 'facts' already presupposed. This does not, of course, mean that the presupposition is untrue: it merely means that, evidentially, it is not yet established. It is a fertile hypothesis, not a firm conclusion. And yet it is also a paradoxical hypothesis: for in general historical analogy would lead us to suppose an opposite result. Who survived better the economic crisis of the Roman Empire, the great magnates or the small landowners? Who weathered the crises of the fourteenth century better, the great land-lords or the gentry?[1] Whose economic condition proved stronger in six-teenth-century Spain—which was perhaps not so different as is vulgarly supposed from sixteenth-century England—the nobles or the *hidalgos*?[2] Who withstood the agrarian crisis of the late nineteenth century in England more successfully, the peers or the gentry? Who, in our own day, can better cope with rising prices and falling gross income, the great landlord who can sell half his estate to adapt the other half, or the small landlord whose property is not so happily divisible? Before accepting the 'plain fact' that Tawney's England witnessed the reverse process, we should perhaps press

[1] See E. Perroy, 'Les Crises du 14ᵉᵐᵉ siècle', in *Annales, Economies, Sociétés, Civilisations* (April–June 1949), p. 181; and cf. M. Campbell, *The English Yeoman* (1942), p. 18.

[2] Cf. R. Altamira, *Historia de España* (Barcelona, 1913), III, 18: 'si en la clase media abundaban las riquezas, solo en la noble se presentaban casos de acumu-laciones extraordinarios.'

the evidence rather more forcibly than he has done, demanding of it not merely what presupposition it will illustrate, but what conclusion it will bear.

II

Let us take Prof. Tawney's statistics first. These at least are hard and factual. Deducing from 'a sample' of some 3300 manors in ten English counties he states that 'out of 730 held by the Crown and the peerage in 1561 some 430 had left them (if new creations are ignored) by 1640, while an additional 400 had been acquired by the gentry'. In consequence, he declares that 'the Crown which in 1561 owned just one-tenth (9 %) of the total, owned in 1640 one-fiftieth (2 %); that the peers held one-eighth (12·6 %) at the first date and (ignoring new creations) one-sixteenth (6·7 %) at the second; and that the share of the gentry had risen from two-thirds (67 %) when the period began, to four-fifths (80 %) at the end of it'. In short, that 'in the counties in question, the landed property of the Crown had diminished...by three-quarters (76 %) and that of the older nobility by approximately one-half (47 %), while that of the gentry had increased by not much less than one-fifth (17·8 %).'

Now whether the figures here given be right or wrong in themselves, I willingly allow, as an incontestable fact, that in the period concerned the landed property of the Crown was substantially diminished. Of that the evidence is overwhelming (although whether the political consequences of this change were quite as significant as is now customarily maintained seems to me questionable).[1] The conclusion for which I feel the need of proof is the conclusion that 'the gentry' gained, and the aristocracy lost, to the extent thus suggested. Some of my reasons for doubt I have already briefly indicated, in another article; but it will be convenient, and I hope therefore allowable, to repeat them here in greater detail. Briefly, they are, first, that the whole method of counting manors as units of wealth is, at the least, unhelpful; secondly, that, even if such a method of calculation were permissible, the distinction between 'aristocracy' and 'gentry' is so entirely arbitrary that no useful conclusions can be based upon it.

For what is a manor? It is not a unit of wealth but a definition of rights. The number of tenants holding of it, the payments and services due from them, the value and extent of the demesne land—all these are subject to the widest variations. This point is so obvious that it needs no emphasis. The second point is more important. For who are the aristocracy, who are the gentry, whose landed property Prof. Tawney has chosen to distinguish and contrast? It will immediately be noticed that he has, for the purpose of calculation, excluded from the peerage all 'new creations'—

---

[1] Our new physiocrats who assume that the Crown, in selling land, was thereby selling its sovereignty, would do well to digest some of the many sensible *Observations on the Land Revenues of the Crown* (1787) by Oliver St John, himself surveyor of Crown lands. 'No civilized state in Europe', says St John, 'draws its public revenues immediately from the rents of lands destined for that purpose'; and he shows that the Crown cannot expect the full value from such lands. And yet the Enlightened Despots of his time were not feeble monarchs.

i.e. (as defined in a footnote) the peers created by James I and Charles I. At first sight this seems a reasonable solution of a real difficulty, for these new peers were, in a sense, 'risen' gentry: the fact that they had risen altogether out of the gentry does not disqualify them as evidence of such 'rise'. With some reason, therefore, Prof. Tawney continued to credit these men to the gentry. But in fact it soon becomes apparent that such an adjustment seriously disconcerts the whole basis of his statistics. For while he has thus defined the aristocracy narrowly, as some sixty particular families who, in the reign of Elizabeth, held titles of honour, he has defined the gentry widely, as all the non-noble private lords of manors—whoever they may have been—in the same counties. He has excluded new peers from the peerage and credited them to the gentry, and has failed to take account of the numerical diminution of the 'old' peers;[1] but what of 'new gentry'—the merchants and yeomen who, throughout that period, were buying manors and whom, by a parity of reasoning, he ought to have excluded from the gentry and credited to the merchants and yeomen? In fact, Prof. Tawney has evidently classed them also as gentry. Thus, while his aristocracy consists of a diminishing group of those families who happened to be noble at the beginning and still noble at the end of the period, his gentry consists both of the gentry who remained gentry throughout the period, and of those men who began as gentry and ended as peers, and of those who began as merchants, yeomen, or anything else, and ended as gentry. No wonder the gentry, thus calculated, appear to 'rise' at the expense of the peerage.

If we thus think it permissible to doubt Prof. Tawney's statistics, what are we to say of his 'stream of comment'? There are two distinct types of comment. On the one hand we have contemporary statements concerning the economic position of individual landlords, from which a modern historian may reasonably make general deductions; on the other hand we have general theories of economic redistribution advanced by contemporary thinkers such as Sir Walter Raleigh, James Harrington, Henry Neville, and others. It will be most convenient to consider the evidence of individual fortunes first, and to postpone to a later stage in the argument the consideration of contemporary theories—which, after all, are only earlier rationalizations of similar evidence. Of this evidence we have a great deal, both from observers and from the parties themselves. Well-informed gossip writers like John Chamberlain, historians like the Earl of Clarendon, testify to the lavish expenditure and large debts of many of their noble contemporaries, who themselves were not reticent on the subject: many a peer, writing to excuse himself from an expensive embassy, or to beg a profitable office or pension, dwelt upon his own financial insufficiency—just as many a gentleman, competing for a county seat or an

---

[1] Twenty peerages whose holders had been summoned to the Parliament of 1559—i.e. nearly one-third of the whole peerage—had become extinct by 1640. Further, among the surviving peerages, titles and unentailed lands sometimes became separated by genealogical, not economic processes. (Mr J. P. Cooper has drawn my attention to several such cases.)

important marriage alliance boasted of his financial capacity. But before drawing any general conclusions from such testimony, we must ask an essential question: do these individual cases of wealth or poverty—however well established—prove the general proposition, viz. that one whole class rose while another whole class declined? In other words, is the evidence of economic difficulty (which may or may not be evidence of economic decline) inseparable from the nobility, and is the evidence of economic advance inseparable from the gentry?

In my opinion the answer is clearly, No. It seems to me that in using the evidence of individual cases, the advocates of these theories have looked for the evidence which they wanted only in the field in which, if found, it would fit those theories. Thus, it is true that many noblemen found themselves in economic difficulties and that some, like the third Lord Vaux, were indeed poor; but is it a fair deduction that their whole order was in similar difficulties? I believe that I have already shown such a deduction to be untrue. And is it a fair deduction that these difficulties were peculiar and exclusive to the nobility? To answer this question we must obviously consider similar evidence in the case of other classes. But this is precisely what Prof. Tawney and his disciples seem to me not to have done. Looking for evidence of economic difficulty only among the peerage, they have indeed found it there; but if they had looked among the gentry they would have found it there too. The Patent Rolls, the Recognizances for Debt, the private bills in Parliament for the sale of lands, the proceedings of the Parliamentary Committees for Compounding, the contemporary family papers and family histories—all show that the difficulties of noble landlords were no different from those of gentry landlords. For one peer who borrows money on recognizance there are a hundred gentlemen. If Sir John Spencer had nine Elizabethan peers on his books, even he—who specialized in the great—had at least twenty-six knights and numerous other gentry. And indeed, why should we expect otherwise? Peers and gentry had, on their different levels, the same problems, the same ambitions, the same conventions, the same tastes. Both were landlords; both had large families; both accepted the rule of primogeniture and the custom of entail; both had to find portions for daughters and younger sons. They built— according to their capacity—similar houses; they were buried in similar tombs. It was an aristocratic age, and the gentry accepted—in general— the standards of value and conduct of the aristocracy. Take a typical history of a typical family of 'rising' Elizabethan gentry: the Holles family. Their prosperity began indeed with a Lord Mayor of London; but by the reign of Elizabeth they were well-established gentry in Lincolnshire. And what was their usual way of life? In the *Memorials* compiled by the family antiquary, we read of fatal extravagance and lavish tastes. Sir William Holles, by his splendid hospitality, 'sent his revenues down the privy house'; Sir George Holles 'maintained a port to the height of what his income would permit him'; Frescheville Holles ruined himself by exchanging Ovid for a kennel of hounds and following 'that magnificent earl of Rutland'; Gervase Holles undid all his economies by building....It is a typical history of 'aristocratic' extravagance.[1] And yet these extravagances, which are alleged to have been ruinous when practised by the aristocracy, are hardly noticed when practised by the gentry. For did not the gentry 'rise'? Did not the Holles family rise so successfully that they bought first a barony, then an earldom, from James I, and ultimately, by the end of the seventeenth century, attained to ducal estate? Other gentry families were less fortunate. The history of the Elizabethan and Jacobean gentry is strewn with their casualties, although Prof. Tawney's searchlight, seeking to illuminate only prosperity among the gentry and aristocratic decline, has seldom lit upon them. If it has, he dismisses them as 'exceptions'. In this essay I shall hope to shed upon them a less flickering light.

If economic problems and expensive tastes thus threatened many of the Elizabethan and Jacobean gentry as well as of the peerage, it is equally true that 'good husbandry' was practised by many of the peerage as well as of the gentry. Prof. Tawney writes as if it were only the gentry who took trouble over their estates. Undoubtedly many did, but this does not necessarily prove that the gentry had a monopoly of good husbandry. As early as 1577, Harrison had noticed the same phenomenon in much greater men: 'Men of great port and countenance', he wrote, 'are so far from suffering their farmers to have any gain at all, that they themselves become graziers, butchers, tanners, sheepmasters, woodmen, *et denique quid non?*'; under James I the Earl of Worcester, head of one of the oldest of noble families, was 'a wonderful great husband and did very much to improve his own estate'; the Earl of Newcastle improved his rent-roll to £22,393 p.a.; and it was a nobleman, not a gentleman, whom Bacon knew, 'that had the greatest audits of any man in my time, a great grazier, a great corn-master, a great lead-man, and so of iron, and a number of the like points of husbandry'.[2]

To this it is sometimes answered that we must distinguish between the 'old' aristocracy of Elizabeth and 'the new Jacobean aristocracy' who, being 'risen gentry', are not admissible as evidence of 'aristocratic' husbandry. But this distinction between 'old' and 'new' peers seems to me just as arbitrary as the distinction between peers and gentry. It is true that Queen Elizabeth, by her parsimony of peerages, broke for a time the continuity of creations, and it is true that the early Stuarts ennobled two merchants and three sons of merchants. But this does not constitute a difference between the Tudor and the Stuart peerages: Charles I, like Elizabeth, interrupted the continuity of creations,[3] and Thomas Cromwell,

---

[1] Gervase Holles, *Memorials of the Holles Family* (Camden Soc. 1937), pp. 42, 78, 215, 229.

[2] William Harrison, *Description of Britain*, II (ed. F. J. Furnivall, 1877), p. 243, and cf. p. 305; Goodman, *Court of James I* (1839), I, 200; Margaret, Duchess of Newcastle, *Life of William Cavendish, Duke of Newcastle* (ed. C. H. Firth, 1907), pp. 75–7; Bacon, *Essays*, 'Of Riches'.

[3] Between March 1629 and November 1640—i.e. in the eleven years of personal rule—only two commoners were raised to the English peerage, and these were both active ministers of the Crown: Sir Francis Cottington, Chancellor of the Exchequer (1631), and Sir John Finch, Lord Keeper (1640).

like Lionel Cranfield, was an ennobled merchant. To call the Elizabethan peerage 'old' as if it represented a different type of landlord from the 'new' Jacobean peerage—an antique caste clinging to obsolete ideas—is absurd. Of the sixty-two members of Elizabeth's peerage in 1560, thirty-seven held titles conferred since the accession of her father, and many of the 'new' Jacobean noble families, like the Cavendishes and the Petres, were indistinguishable in their origins from 'old' Tudor families like the Russells and the Wriothesleys. All had risen as officials of Henry VIII: if some had been ennobled at the time and some had to wait sixty years, that does not constitute a significant difference. In fact, the Tudor peers, like the Stuart peers, were largely self-made men. If the former often had economic difficulties and the latter often prospered, this was not due to a difference of class-mentality but to a difference of economic conditions. After 1600 conditions improved; and the improvement was exploited just as fully by really old noble families like the Somersets, Talbots and·Howards as by 'new' noble families like the Cavendishes, Spencers and Montagus.

Thus if we examine the evidence fairly, unprejudiced by the artificial distinction between peers and commoners, we find that the same sort of evidence which shows extravagant habits and economic difficulties among the nobility shows also similar habits and similar difficulties among the gentry, and the same sort of evidence which shows improvement and good husbandry among the gentry shows similar achievements among the nobility. It is not proper to write off improving peers and decaying gentry as exceptions to the rule until some evidence has been produced to prove the rule. The whole distinction between the peerage and gentry, upon which so much has been built, becomes again what it has always been in England, a distinction of nomenclature and legal rights, not a difference of either habits of mind or economic practice; and the theory that, because of such differences, one class—the peerage—declined while the other—the gentry—'rose' is by definition untenable.

III

I thus conclude that Prof. Tawney's theory of the rise of the gentry at the expense of a declining peerage is a mistaken formulation. If I am right in this, it may seem unnecessary to go on to the second stage of the investigation: the examination of the cause which he has assigned to the phenomenon he has presupposed. But this, I think, would be too radical. Prof. Tawney may have mistaken the nature of the phenomenon and incorrectly expressed it. But there nevertheless is a phenomenon, which may still be called 'the rise of the gentry', and this phenomenon, even if it needs to be differently stated, still needs to be explained. The rising class may not have been 'the gentry' as distinct from 'the peerage'; but certain families within the landlord class—whether peers or gentry—undoubtedly did prosper and acquired, through their political machine the Houses of Parliament, political power at the expense of the Crown. The question is, who were these families, and to what did they owe their prosperity? In particular, did they, as Prof. Tawney has supposed (it is the essential part of his thesis), owe their rise to 'husbandry', to the exploitation of new opportunities and new techniques in the direct management of land— opportunities and techniques which, by a further refinement of his theory, he supposes to have been more applicable to small than to large estates?

At this point it is necessary to define the field of inquiry. I am concerned with the phenomenon which Prof. Tawney has described as 'the rise of the gentry', and which I would prefer to re-define as the rise *within* the gentry of certain families. I am not concerned with the rise *into* the gentry of successful yeomen. The fact of that rise seems incontestable. It was noted at the time;[1] it has been analysed in detail on a local basis by Dr Hoskins[2] and on a national basis by Prof. Campbell.[3] Yeomen, farming their lands directly, often built up properties 'worth three or four squires put together' and were found 'able yearly to dispend betwixt 3 and 5 hundred pounds'. They bought lands from peers and gentry, lent them money, and sometimes, in a few generations, replaced them in their seats. But an essential condition of the rise of a yeoman was that he was a yeoman, 'a gentlemen in ore' as Fuller called him, but not yet a gentleman. He had yeoman tastes, yeoman methods, yeoman habits. He did not have to keep up the 'port' of a gentleman; he did not entertain the ambitions of a gentleman; and half his prosperity was due to this saving. He sold his surplus at rising prices, and having food and clothing from his farm, and few other expenses save his rent, was alone, among the merely landed classes, exempt 'from the costly charge of these unfaithful times'.[4] A gentleman who eschewed gentry tastes and ambitions and lived like a yeoman, like Robert Loder, could of course similarly thrive.[5] Further, not being tenants-in-chief, yeomen were exempt from some of the more burdensome taxes of the gentry. Thus yeomen, from the direct profits of land, undoubtedly 'rose'; but this does not mean that the gentry could or did similarly rise, or that once yeomen had become gentry they could continue to rise, by the same methods, above the consequence of a rich farmer. The 'rising' gentry are not gentry like Robert Loder, the solitary instance whom Prof. Tawney presents as a universal type. Robert Loder did not rise. He stayed where he was, a prosperous farmer of a steady 150 acres with a steady net income of £200–£300 p.a. The 'rising' gentry on the other hand (even by Prof. Tawney's own definition of them) are quite different. They are real gentry with gentry tastes and gentry ambitions, paying gentry taxes and filling gentry offices: men of 'county families' who pushed their way into Parliament, rose to the peerage, and became not merely the rural basis but the political *élite* of England. The fact that yeomen grew into gentry through direct agriculture does not mean that

---

[1] W. Harrison, *Description of Britain*, II (ed. F. J. Furnivall, 1877), p. 133.
[2] 'The Leicestershire Farmer in the 16th Century', in *Essays in Leicestershire History* (1950).
[3] Mildred Campbell, *The English Yeoman* (Yale, 1942).
[4] Campbell, *op. cit.* p. 187.
[5] *Robert Loder's Farm Accounts* (Camden Soc. 1936).

gentry could grow into peers by the same process. A gentleman, said Sir Thomas Smith, is one that can bear 'the port, charge and countenance of a gentleman'. The yeomen rose precisely because they eschewed that costly apparatus. The invocation of yeomen methods to explain the rise of the gentry is an inadmissible analogy.

Who then were the rising families? Certainly the whole gentry class did not rise—indeed there is plenty of evidence of decline within it. There were, according to Dr Hoskins, 'between 360 and 400 indisputable gentry in Devon' in the early seventeenth-century,[1] but only a handful of these 'rose'; and the same generalization can be extended to the whole of England. When we speak of the 'rising' gentry we mean, in fact, a small minority who rose within and sometimes out of the class in which the great majority of their brethren were content or obliged to remain more or less stationary. If we can isolate these families, or at least isolate a sufficient number of agreed representatives of them, we shall be in a position to begin an inquiry into the cause of such rise: an inquiry which may either confirm or modify or perhaps even reverse Prof. Tawney's theories.

How shall we begin to isolate the 'rising' families? One obvious group at once presents itself. The new peers created by James I and Charles I are admitted by Prof. Tawney to have been 'risen' gentry, and I readily accept this definition. They are also a convenient group, being of manageable size and clearly defined frontiers. For several years before 1603 and after 1629 creations were negligible, but in those twenty-six years the English peerage was doubled in size by the elevation of seventy-two commoners: forty-six by James I, twenty-six by Charles I. Who were these commoners and to what economic activity did they owe the wealth which enabled them to sustain, and sometimes to purchase, their new dignities?

Almost without exception they were office-holders. Cecils and Howards, Herberts and Villiers and their numerous kindred—there is no need to pry closely into the origins of those new windfalls. They were the great court-fortunes; beneath them came the lesser, but still considerable, fortunes that could be derived from offices in the household, the army, and—particularly—the law. To divide the new Stuart peers exactly into these categories is impossible, for many were pluralists; but between these categories at least 90 % of them can be easily and obviously accounted for. The majority, like Sir Robert Sidney, Sir William Knollys, Sir Edward Wotton, Sir John Digby, had already become rich through office when their status was confirmed by their new titles. Others, to whom peerages were a sign of sudden favour, like Sir Henry Rich or Sir Henry Danvers or the Villiers family, at once received court offices to sustain their new dignities. Even those whose titles were the result neither of peculiar service nor of peculiar favour, but of open purchase, had generally acquired the ability to pay from offices or perhaps trade rather than from land. Sir John Roper paid £10,000 for the barony of Teynham. He could afford to do so. His office of Clerk of Enrolments of the Kings Bench was evidently

---

[1] 'The Estates of the Caroline Gentry' in W. G. Hoskins and H. P. R. Finberg, *Devonshire Studies* (1952).

worth some £3500 p.a. Three successive royal favourites intrigued for the succession to it, and for arranging its reversion to the Duke of Buckingham a Lord Chief Justice received £500 p.a. out of it as a broker's fee.[1] Sir John Holles also paid £10,000 for the barony of Houghton, and another £5000 for the Earldom of Clare. It is true he was noted for his economies, 'nothing liberal: no man living more ready to oblige by his interest and endeavours, but not at all by his purse'; but it was not only land that he husbanded. If, by the end of his life, he had 'advanced his estate to near £8000 *per annum*', it was partly thanks to a pension from Queen Elizabeth and the office of Comptroller of the Household to the Prince of Wales. When the Prince died, Holles declared that his hopes and fortunes lay in the grave with him, and he angled and wangled for new offices in its stead. It was as Secretary of State or Lord Deputy of Ireland, not only as a resident landlord in Nottinghamshire, that he looked to increase his fortune.[2] Sir Philip Stanhope was another who paid £10,000 for a barony. The whole Stanhope family was indeed rising at that time, but not through new methods of agriculture. The family fortune had been made in the politics of Protector Somerset; it had been swollen in the next generation by offices in church, law, household, and administration. Sir John Stanhope, Master of the Posts, member of the Council in the North, Treasurer of the Chamber to Queen Elizabeth, Vice-Chamberlain to King James, had already acquired a Jacobean peerage; his brother, Sir Edward Stanhope, Master of Requests, Chancellor of the diocese of London, vicar-general of the Archbishop of Canterbury, prebendary of York, canon of St Paul's cathedral, *alias* 'rich Dr Stanhope' the moneylender, 'estant de £40,000 wealth et de nul expence' as another lawyer sourly described him,[3] dying childless, enriched his brothers' families. Yet another of his brothers was surveyor of the Duchy of Lancaster, Treasurer of Gray's Inn, Recorder of Doncaster, member of the Council in the North. No new agricultural technique was necessary to buy peerages for the Stanhope family. Another venal peerage was that of the Finch family. In 1623 the widow of Sir Moyle Finch, 'for £12,000 given to the Duke and Duchess of Richmond', was created Viscountess Maidstone. But whence did this opulence come? Not—as far as the evidence goes—from improved agricultural economy. Lady Finch was the sole daughter and heir of that great official pluralist Sir Thomas Heneage, Treasurer of the Queen's Chamber, vice-chamberlain of the Household, Paymaster of the Forces, Chancellor of the Duchy of Lancaster, etc., etc.... Thus almost every peerage in the period 1603–29 can be shown in turn to have rested, economically, not on land but on offices. The few exceptions are mainly

[1] The great competition for Sir John Roper's office may be followed in the Cecil Papers and in the State Papers (Domestic), and in Whitelocke's *Liber Famelicus* (Camden Soc. 1858).

[2] Holles, *Memorials of the Holles Family* (Camden Soc. 1937), pp. 95, 112–14, 191, 250.

[3] *Diary of Roger Wilbraham* (Camden Miscellany, 1902), x, 99. Dr Stanhope's moneylending activities are recorded in P.R.O. Recognizances for Debt.

based not on land but on trade. Sir Baptist Hicks, Viscount Camden, was a clothier. Sir William Craven, Lord Craven, was the son of a clothier. Sir Paul Bayning based his viscountcy on his father's success as an East India merchant. All these men were also royal officials in so far as they were not merely private merchants but also government financiers. Lionel Cranfield, Earl of Middlesex, was similarly both merchant and minister. Lord Robartes, an involuntary venal peer—he was forced by the Duke of Buckingham to purchase a barony for £10,000—was a tin magnate.

Do none of the new peers then represent the landed fortunes of agriculturally minded squires? We cannot exclude some possibilities. The Spencers of Althorp were certainly great sheep farmers (though mercantile and legal wealth was also infused by marriage into the family); and it may well be that land was to them not only the expression and evidence of their great wealth but also its principal source. But apart from this one family is there a single instance, among the new peers created by the early Stuarts, of a fortune based solely or even mainly on the profits of land? As far as positive evidence is concerned, I can find none. There are indeed some families to whom no great offices or mercantile successes or spectacular marriages can be ascribed, and who were yet able to buy or accept new titles. I do not know how Sir Robert Dormer of Wing, or Sir Francis Leake of Scarsdale, raised the money necessary for the purchase of their titles. Perhaps it was by agricultural improvement. The Leakes were certainly known as depopulators—which is not necessarily the same as improvers—and Sir Francis, the new peer, was accused of unreasonable economy.[1] Then there were the Tuftons, Earls of Thanet, whose estate, by 1642, was worth £10,000 p.a. Perhaps it was good estate-management which built up this great fortune—although a series of marriages into legal and political families must at least have helped.[2] Sir Robert Pierrepont, too, created Earl of Kingston, 'a man of vast estate and no less covetous', 'of great fortune and great parsimony', who spent £1000 p.a. buying land, may well have derived his increased wealth from land-management (for the family had in the past been great enclosers);[3] just as the Petre family undoubtedly raised the value of their estates—originally acquired through office—by prudent management.[4] On the other hand they may not; and even if they did, it may have been not by demesne-farming, but (as in the case of the Petres) by raising of rents and administrative economy. And if so—if in fact it was raising of rents not direct management as entrepreneurs that enriched these men—then it would seem to follow that the great landlords with more rents to raise would be in a better not a worse position

---

[1] *V.C.H. Notts*, II, 282; Clarendon, *History of the Rebellion* (ed. 1843), pp. 301–2.

[2] *Calendar of the Committee for Compounding*, p. 839; R. Pocock, *Memorials of the Family of Tufton* (Gravesend, 1800).

[3] Lucy Hutchinson, *Memoir of Colonel Hutchinson* (ed. Everyman), p. 93; Clarendon, *History of the Rebellion* (1843), pp. 301–2. William Pierrepont, in the sixteenth century, had converted 220 acres at Holme Pierrepont from arable and meadow to pasture (*V.C.H. Notts*, II, 281).

[4] For this and other evidence about the Petre estates I am indebted to the valuable thesis of Mr W. R. Emerson, *The Petre Estates 1540–1640*.

than the small. However, in the absence of evidence about these families I would prefer not to base any general theory on so precarious an assumption. There are plenty of other possibilities; and until they have been disposed of, I would prefer to say that we do not know.

Thus in an analysis of the 'new' peerage I find no adequate support for Prof. Tawney's theory. Rather I conclude that whereas many families indubitably increased the yield of their lands, the great new fortunes were almost invariably made either by offices or in trade. Indeed, I would go further and say that between 1540 and 1640 land alone, without the help of offices or trade, even if it were improved, was hardly capable of causing the significant rise of any but a most exceptional family. For against the increased rents shown on estate accounts in this period must be placed the decline in the value of money. Economists seem generally agreed that the value of money, by 1640, had declined to one-third of the value which it had had in 1540; on the other hand, only the best managed estates were so improved in the same period that they yielded to the landlord at the end of it three times the rent which they had yielded at the beginning. It would therefore seem logical to assume that land was at best a long-term investment, yielding only a marginal profit. Indeed, in the reign of Elizabeth, when the fall in the value of money continued steep and the great rise in rents had not yet begun, the whole position of the landowning classes must sometimes have seemed perilous; and although, after 1590, rentals seem generally to have risen, the general economic depression of the following decade must have postponed recovery, for many families, into the next reign. In these circumstances to doubt whether the mere management of land could raise a family from one social class into another would seem not a 'paradox' but common sense.

Now this general conclusion about the economic basis of social advance in the sixteenth century, which I have so far deduced only from one category of evidence—the evidence of the new peerage—can, I think, be similarly deduced by any other method of analysis. Take, for instance, Prof. Tawney's somewhat rhetorical picture of the dissolution of large estates: 'as each over-rigged vessel went on the rocks, the patient watchers on the shore'—i.e. the gentry—'brought home fresh flotsam from the wreck'. Let us reduce this metaphor to fact by actually examining one of these shipwrecks. In the 1580's the Earl of Oxford—not because of typical 'aristocratic' land-management but through exceptional and eccentric extravagance—sold a number of manors in Essex.[1] And who were the purchasers? Gentry? Some of them indeed have the words 'gent' or 'esquire' after their names—for they were indeed lords of manors in the county; but when we trace them further they generally change this character. Incidentally they may be classed as gentry, but they are not 'mere gentry', i.e. country squires who derive their income exclusively from land and can base their 'rise' exclusively on their more direct and professional management of it. Mr Skinner, the purchaser of Lanham,

[1] The manors and their purchasers are given in a document printed by Strype, *Annals* (1824), III, ii, 191.

Castle Camps and Fulmer, was a London merchant who died as Lord
Mayor; Mr Glascock, squire of Great Dunmow and other manors, who
bought Wivenhoe, Bentley, Baterswick and New Year's Farm, was also
a London merchant; Israel Amys, squire of Tilbury Hall, was the Earl's
surveyor; Mr Hubberd, the new lord of Stansted Mountfichet (which he
would soon sell to a great London merchant, Sir Thomas Middleton), was
one of the six clerks in Chancery; John Mabbe, the purchaser of Nether
and Little Yeldam, was a London goldsmith; William Tiffin, the new
owner of Wakes Hall, was a common lawyer.... Clearly it was not merely
by new methods of agriculture that these men were enabled thus to increase their property, adding new acres to old. Wherever one looks the
general conclusion is the same. In 1603 Lord Cobham lost his estates, not
through managerial inefficiency but through a charge of treason. What
happened to them? Theoretically they passed into gentry hands—into the
hands of Cobham's cousin, Duke Brooke esq. of Temple Combe, Somerset,
who secured the right to buy the entailed estates from the Crown for a
total sum of £11,500. But what in fact happened? In fact Duke Brooke,
being a mere gentleman, was unable to raise this sum without recourse to
the moneylenders. The first instalment of £5000 he borrowed from
Alexander Prescott, citizen and goldsmith of London; the second instalment of £3250 from the great clothier and moneylender Sir John Spencer;
the third instalment was raised, after Duke Brooke's death, by his brother
and heir Charles Brooke, from Peter van Lore, the naturalized Dutch
financier, and the professional moneylender Thomas Sutton. By this time
a new figure has appeared on the scene: the unsteady credit of the Brookes
is supported by Sir John Daccombe, chancellor of the exchequer and man
of affairs for Robert Cecil, Earl of Salisbury. In the end, few if any of the
Cobham lands remained with the Brookes. The goldsmith, Alexander
Prescott, obtained, in repayment of his loan, the Essex estates of Radwinter
and Bendish; the merchant, Sir John Spencer, obtained, in repayment of
his loan, the Bedfordshire estate of Newnham Priory; the chancellor, Sir
John Daccombe, obtained the Kentish estates of Maidstone Abbey; and
when Charles Brooke died in 1610, he left the rest of his lands to the Earl
of Salisbury, who, by the terms of the will, was to pay off the debts and
mortgages thereon. Once again the mere gentry are unable to use their
opportunities: the beneficiaries of change are always the office-holders and
the merchants.[1] In fact, from the time when the monastery lands went not
to all the local gentry but only to those few who happened, through their
offices, to be connected with the court, to the time when the squandered
Church and Crown lands were sold, during the Revolution, to syndicates
of City merchants and the new office-holders of the Army and its Rump
Parliament, the story is always the same. Even Prof. Tawney's own lists
of gentry are almost always—when he correctly describes them as 'rising'

---

[1] The history of these changes can be traced in Hist. MSS. Comm., Marquess
of Salisbury, xvi, 123, 334, 352; xvii, 539; xviii, 59, 165; P.R.O. Recognizances
for Debt; Morant, *Essex*, II, 535, 537; *V.C.H. Bedfordshire*, III, 298–9; Frederick
Brown, *Abstracts of Somersetshire Wills*, I, 4; Cal. S.P. Dom. (1611–18), p. 38.

—lists not of mere squires whose income must be ascribed to rents and agriculture, but of lawyers, officials, or merchants, whose profits came from quite different sources. Whom does he name as fortunate lessees of under-rented Crown lands? 'Sir William Cecil, Sir Thomas Smith, Anthony Brown (Justice of the Common Pleas), David Lewis (Judge of the Court of Admiralty), Sir Francis Knollys....' Legally these men were indeed gentry, for they were landlords who were not peers; but economically they do not represent the 'mere gentry' and cannot properly be cited as evidence of their rise: they were officials.

Another criterion of the 'rising' families in this period can be provided by the great houses with which successful families signalized—and some-times terminated—their prosperity. It was an age of competitive domestic architecture: 'No kingdom in the world', wrote Bishop Goodman of the reign of James I, 'spent so much in building as we did in his time'; and the surviving monuments of that architectural mania are still the most vivid and unmistakable relics of their age. But what was the financial basis of those great houses? Dr Hoskins, in his admirable essay on 'the Deserted Villages of Leicestershire', has summarized the view which Prof. Tawney has made classical. 'In many of these places', he writes, speaking of the sites of sixteenth-century enclosures, 'a great house still stands as a monu-ment to the wealth that enclosure had created for the few: Quenby and Baggrave, Lowesby and Stanford, Withcote, Noseley and Brooksby'; and the ruined or extinct houses at Knaptoft, Foston, Elmesthorpe and Rag-dale are implicitly ascribed to the same fortunes.[1] But what is the evidence for such statements? Landlords enclosed, villages shrank and disappeared, certain families became rich. These three statements may all be separately true, but it does not necessarily follow that the rise of the families con-cerned was the direct consequence of the enclosure, or that their houses (many of which were anyway built 150 years later) illustrate such profits. In fact, the builder of Quenby, George Ashby, had married the heiress of George Bennett, citizen and salter of London, one of those rich merchants whose advance in the Midlands so alarmed the local gentry, and the £12,000 which was spent on the house almost certainly came from mer-cantile not agricultural profits. The Smiths of Withcote were restored to wealth under Elizabeth by the mercantile fortune of a younger son of the family, Ambrose Smith of Cheapside, silkman to the Queen.[2] The Caves, squires of Baggrave and Stanford, were a family of well-rewarded Reforma-tion officials. Neither the Villiers of Brooksby nor the Harringtons and their successors the Cokaynes of Elmesthorpe depended on agriculture for their prosperity. The Faunts of Foston established themselves by the law. In fact, an instance has yet to be given of a great house in Leicestershire which can safely be described as a monument to the wealth created by enclosure in the period before 1660.

Turning from the unpretending houses of a sample county to the great houses of England, we find the same conclusions forced upon us. We have

[1] W. G. Hoskins, *Essays in Leicestershire History* (1950), p. 101.
[2] Nichols, *Leicestershire*, II, 388.

only to collect the instances for the answer to appear. Chatsworth and Hinchingbrooke, Hatfield and Audley End, Burghley House, Knole, Warwick Castle (on which Sir Fulke Greville spent 'at least £20,000'),[1] Kirby and Holdenby, Wilton, Salden, Apethorpe, Cobham, Bramshill and many others were built on the profits of administration; Montacute and Gorhambury, Blickling and Loseley, Lynsted and Doddington illustrated the profits of law; Chastleton and East Riddlesden more modestly advertised mercantile fortunes; Temple Newsam blazoned the mushroom wealth of a new financier. Others—like Longford and Lulworth—can be ascribed to the windfalls of successful marriage. But what houses were built, in that great epoch of building, on the profits of land? Rushton? Perhaps—but it anyway ruined its builder. Wollaton? Possibly—though Sir Francis Willoughby's land produced, with its coal and iron, more profitable crops than cereals or even sheep; and it too—combined with the cost of a senile marriage—nearly ruined his family. At the beginning of the reign of Elizabeth, Sir Francis Willoughby's estate was 'known both to Her Majesty and the whole Council to be nothing inferior to the best'; by the end of it, when, 'upon a vain ostentation of his wealth', he had built that architectural monstrosity, his heir inherited a diminished estate, encumbered with long leases, mortgages, 'divers great annuities', bonds and statutes of infinite value', and £21,000 of debt.[2] Such was the consequence of building on the slender foundation of even metalliferous land. Of some seventy great Elizabethan and Jacobean houses whose economic foundations I have examined only one—Althorp—seems to have been built successfully on a largely landed fortune; the rest, like the new peerages and the new estates, were founded and sustained usually on offices, sometimes on trade.

Not every successful man built himself a great house; but he made, as a rule, careful provision for his own burial: in his will he dictated, or his heirs decided for him, the number of mourners, the scale of the feast, the cost and style of the commemorative tomb. Of these great pageants, wherewith, in an age that solemnized mortality, dynasties delighted—even against the wishes of the deceased—to commemorate their own stages, only the tombs now survive: but what tombs they are! In the sixteenth century the art of the monumental mason was required in England as never before, and until a native school was prepared to take over, foreign artists—Italians, Huguenots, Flemings—converged to supply the demand. For it was not now great peers and bishops only who insisted on dominating, after death, their local churches: newly prosperous gentry were now equally exacting. In every English county the leading families can be traced, in village churches, by their sumptuous effigies and panegyrical inscriptions, whose style and splendour, according to the accepted rules of that competitive but still carefully hierarchical age, is a safe indication of status and quality; for 'sepulchres', as a contemporary declared, 'should be made according to the quality and degree of the persons deceased, that

---

[1] Sir W. Dugdale, *The Antiquities of Warwickshire* (1656), p. 343.
[2] Hist. MSS. Comm. Lord Middleton, pp. 538, 583–5, 588–9, 619; Camden, *Britannia* (1637), p. 547.

by the tomb everyone might be discerned of what rank he was living'.[1]
And who are these gentry families who now judged themselves worthy to
usurp the place of peers and bishops and old crusaders? They may not be
known to national history, or easily traceable in its records, but those who
follow Prof. Tawney's own advice, to lay aside their books in favour of
their boots, can soon discover them in their own complacent lapidary
autobiographies. Successful courtiers, like the Hobys whose splendid
monuments dazzle the parishioners of Bisham (appropriately, Sir Thomas
Hoby translated for his fellow-countrymen *the Courtier* of Castiglione)';
lawyers like Lord Chief Justice Popham or Chief Baron Tanfield who rest
proudly under their canopies in the churches of Wellington and Burford;
merchants like Sir Thomas Middleton at Stansted Mountfichet, and
numerous others whose gilded effigies can be found in City churches;
privileged speculators like the notorious monopolist Sir Giles Mompesson,
who converses with his wife in dignified ease at Lydiard Tregoze—these
are the standard types: but where are the 'mere gentry'? Of all types,
says the greatest expert on this subject,[2] the country gentleman is the
rarest. Perhaps he was a recusant, who kept away from his parish church—
and yet rich recusants, like the Ropers, with their great legal fortune, set
up in the church of Lynsted some of the most elegant of all such monuments. Perhaps he was a puritan, who despised such 'superfluous expense
upon the sepulchres of the dead'—and yet rich puritans did not disdain
them—like Sir Christopher Packe, who offered Cromwell the crown and
now still swoons, in expensive marble and a lord mayor's robes, in the
church of Prestwold; nor did the puritan republic, when it could command
public money, know any better way to honour its dead founders: in
Westminster Abbey, that 'dormitory of kings', it voted to Henry Ireton
'a magnificent monument at the public charge', and to Oliver Cromwell
himself a funeral of unparalleled magnificence and a vast and costly
tomb.[3] If other puritan gentry despised such 'pompous and expensive
vanities'[4] that was no doubt because their puritanism, like the recusancy
of so many gentry recusants, was a reflexion of their comparative poverty.
The mere gentry, the *country* gentry, hated what they could not afford: it
was the rich official gentry, the *court* gentry, linked by office or trade with
London, the centre alike of taste and manufacture,[5] who were able thus
to immortalize themselves.

[1] Weever, *Funeral Monuments* (1631), §3, quoted in K. A. Esdaile, *English
Church Monuments* (1946), p. 138.

[2] K. A. Esdaile, *op. cit.* p. 94.

[3] Cromwell's funeral (according to Heath, *Chronicle* (1663), p. 739) cost
£60,000. The funeral of James I, 'the greatest indeed that ever was known in
England' was said to have cost £50,000 (*Letters of John Chamberlain*, ed. McClure,
II, 616).

[4] Ludlow, *Memoirs* (ed. C. H. Firth, 1894), I, 295.

[5] That London was the centre of such manufacture, at least after 1550, is
clearly shown by Mrs Esdaile (*op. cit.* p. 45). In counties where the gentry were
poor and had no contact with London, such monuments are rare—e.g. in
Northumberland, where I only know of a few merchant tombs in Newcastle-
upon-Tyne.

But perhaps the fairest means of identifying Prof. Tawney's 'rising' families is not merely to select the possessors of new titles and new estates, or the builders of great houses and great tombs, but to take the families actually cited in evidence by Prof. Tawney himself: the families whose rise, ascribed by him to agricultural improvement, is cited by him as symptomatic of the similar rise of their whole class. Who are these families and what general conclusions does their history in fact illustrate? In fact, if we examine those very families which Prof. Tawney has himself named as the profiteers of agriculture, we find (as it seems to me) exactly the same results as we have already reached by other methods of analysis. In almost every case where evidence is attainable that evidence shows that the rise of these families was accompanied by the tenure of offices or the profits of trade; and, further, that when these advantages were withdrawn, and the families concerned were driven back into absolute dependence upon land, they at once apprehended and often experienced not a rise but a decline.

Thus, to illustrate the thesis that monastic lands, originally granted to noblemen and officials, quickly slid into the more tenacious grasp of more agriculturally minded local gentry, Prof. Tawney gives evidence of many transfers of land from one owner to another but nowhere shows that these transfers were from one class to another. Indeed, some of his instances are definitely contrary to his thesis. Thus he states that 'the lands of Sir Thomas Gresham came by marriage to the Thynnes and those of Lord Clinton and Sir Robert Tyrwhitt to the Heydons'. Of these instances the former proves little, since Gresham was a merchant and marriage is not evidence of insolvency; the latter merely shows one gentry family replacing another. For who were the Tyrwhitts and the Heydons? Their rise and decline perfectly illustrates the thesis which I would oppose to that of Prof. Tawney, viz. that offices, not land, were the usual source of the 'rise' of families and that loss of office, entailing exclusive dependence on land, was often the prelude to economic decline. The Tyrwhitts were a successful Lincolnshire family, long sustained by legal and official posts, sheriffs of the county, knights of the shire. Sir Robert Tyrwhitt, who died in 1575, was a member of Elizabeth's household, and his wife had been her governess. He acquired the site and property of Thornton Abbey (which Henry VIII had intended for a college), and on his death left lands in Lincolnshire, worth £250 p.a., in Sussex, worth £141 p.a., and other lands in Yorkshire and Essex. This good fortune did not last. By the end of the sixteenth century the family, suspected of popery and in disgrace with the Queen, had lost contact with the refreshing perquisites of office, and seeking to maintain, in spite of that weakness, the 'port' necessary to such a 'worshipful ancient family', was rapidly declining. The new Sir Robert Tyrwhitt borrowed money from Thomas Sutton and from the money-lending lawyers Sir John Hele, Sir Edward Stanhope and Sir Julius Caesar. In 1598 he sold his estate of Buslingthorpe to Thomas Sutton; in 1602 he sold Thornton Abbey to Sir Vincent Skinner, officer of the Receipt of Exchequer; in 1604 another property—the manor of Nettleton near Caistor—passed to Sutton; by 1611 Tyrwhitt owed money to Sir Baptist

Hicks, and his surviving bonds to Sutton were classed by Sutton's executors in the category of debts 'some of them doubtful, some desperate'. By 1621 Kettleby had gone. By the time of the Civil War the family, now firm recusants, was so reduced that they could compound for their whole estate at £400.[1]

The same general conclusion is illustrated by the Norfolk family of Heydon. Their prosperity had been founded in the fifteenth century by a lawyer, John Heydon, who 'much advanced the estate and fortunes of his family, being a feoffee and trustee to most of the great estates in that county'. Thus law and stewardship, not agriculture, was the basis of the rise of the Heydons, which John Heydon and his son Sir Henry Heydon (steward to the household of the Duchess of York) illustrated by the building of their new family seats, the 'spacious sumptuous pile' of Baconsthorpe and the great house at Saxlingham. There, in the middle of the century, Sir Christopher Heydon, enriched with monastic lands, displayed his 'remarkable hospitality, equal to his ample estate'. A generation later, when the Heydons no longer ranked among the official families, what a difference we find! Sir Christopher Heydon's two grandsons, Sir Christopher and Sir John, sought to continue expensive habits without the essential economic basis. Decayed and disreputable, notorious for duals and brawls, 'infamy, grief, and other inconveniences', they became bywords in court and country. In vain their great neighbour, Sir Edward Coke, exerted his influence 'to repair the fortunes of Sir Christopher Heydon' and his brother John 'a poor gentleman of Norfolk...as poor as ever Irus was'. By December 1600 Baconsthorpe was mortgaged; in February 1601 the two brothers, deep in debt, appeared in the streets of London with that leader of the decayed, excluded gentry of England, the Earl of Essex. Thereafter the debts mounted (increased by a fine of £2000 for participation in the revolt); in vain Sir Christopher Heydon begged for offices or relief—the farm of the customs of Norfolk, a quillet of escheated lands. By 1609 he owed £2500 to Thomas Sutton alone. By 1614 his creditors had closed upon him and all his lands were sold.[2]

Another family named by Prof. Tawney as evidence of 'rising' gentry is that of Throckmorton. A closer glance at the history of this family is equally instructive. In the first half of the sixteenth century they indeed rose—through offices. Sir Robert Throckmorton was a Privy Councillor to Henry VII; his son, Sir George Throckmorton, was a courtier of Henry VIII, connected by marriage with Queen Katherine Parr, steward

[1] R. P. Tyrwhitt, *Notices and Remains of the Family of Tyrwhitt* (revised edition, 1872); papers of Thomas Sutton preserved at the Charterhouse, London (hereafter referred to as Charterhouse MSS.); information kindly supplied by Mr P. M. Tillott.

[2] The rise and decline of the Heydon family can be traced in F. Blomefield, *Topographical History of Norfolk* (1739–75), v, 504; IX, 434; Sir William Heydon's monument in Baconsthorpe church; Hist. MSS. Comm., Gawdy, 69, 71–2, 82, 96, 98; *ibid.* Marquess of Salisbury, xi, 44, 88, 214; xv, 72; xvii, 68; Cal. S.P. Dom. (1603–10), p. 377; Notestein, Relf and Simpson, *Parliamentary Debates 1621* (1935), VI, 103 and references there cited.

of the Priory of Studley, commissioner for Warwickshire at the Dissolution of the Monasteries, and—as a natural consequence—grantee of the Warwickshire lands of Studley Priory. Two of Sir George's sons continued this profitable connexion with government. Sir Nicholas Throckmorton, brought up in the household of the Queen, was Knight of the Privy Chamber, Treasurer of the Mint, Chief Butler to Queen Elizabeth, Chamberlain of the Exchequer; his brother Sir John Throckmorton was Master of Requests, for twenty-three years Chief Justice of Chester and a member of the Council of Wales. So far—it is as far as the offices go—all is well. But in the next generation all is changed. Sir Arthur Throckmorton indeed continues at Paulerspury, Northants, the 'splendid housekeeping' of his father 'the great Sir Nicholas Throckmorton';[1] but how different is the fate of the rest of the family, cut off by recusancy from the offices on which the family had risen! The two sons of Sir John Throckmorton are desperate conspirators for Mary Queen of Scots. A generation later six members of the family are among the thirteen conspirators in that desperate venture of the impoverished recusant gentry: the Gunpowder Plot.

One of these is Francis Tresham, himself the representative of another of Prof. Tawney's 'rising' families. Indeed Sir Thomas Tresham seems to be the only instance of a squire who is explicitly described by Prof. Tawney as 'rising' by specified agricultural techniques: the sole instance of a practice which all other gentry families are loosely said to illustrate. Did he not sell 'everything, from rabbits supplied on contract to a poulterer in Gracechurch Street, to wool to the value of £1000 a year'? But what was the result of these harmless activities? Office had indeed raised the Treshams —Sir Thomas's father had been the last Prior of St John of Jerusalem—but recusancy after 1580 had made office no longer attainable to the family. Nevertheless, on the mere basis of land, they had sought to maintain the standards of their class, building a gigantic house and sprinkling Northamptonshire with elaborate architectural conceits. A lawyer, a household officer, a politician might do these things and survive: a mere landlord could not. By 1591 Sir Thomas Tresham had begun to mortgage his lands; by 1593 he had begun to sell; from 1594 we have records of his debts to Thomas Sutton, John Robinson and other merchants and moneylenders; in 1601 his son Francis—his allowance reduced to £100 p.a. and his keep— took part in Essex's rising and involved Sir Thomas in a fine of £2000 and a bribe of £1000 to Lady Katherine Howard to preserve him from anything worse. By 1605 Francis Tresham was involved in the Gunpowder Plot and died in the Tower. His brother, Sir Lewis Tresham, still struggled to maintain the old style of life at Rushton; but not for long. In 1607 he sought relief from alderman Cokayne. That—as for so many Midland gentry—was the beginning of the end. In 1616 alderman Cokayne cancelled bonds of Sir Lewis Tresham to the value of some £28,000 and Sir Thomas Tresham's great house at Rushton with its emblematic lodges and

---

[1] Inscription on his tomb in Paulerspury church, Northants.

symbolic follies became one of the seats of the new dynasty of Cokayne, viscounts Cullen.[1]

It may be objected that many of these are recusants, and that recusancy, not lack of office, was the cause of their decline. I can only answer, first, that I have not chosen them for that reason: I have taken them because Prof. Tawney has named them as instances of 'rising' families; and, secondly, that the objection anyway seems to me irrelevant; for although work remains to be done on the economic consequences of recusancy, and any generalizations on that subject must therefore be tentative, it seems to me that the chief economic disadvantage of recusancy was not the imposition of fines, irregularly exacted, but the continuous exclusion from office which it almost necessarily entailed. Some country gentry were excluded from office by chance or incompetence, some were excluded, or sanctified their exclusion, by choice: the effect was the same. Take an undeniably protestant family, the Cromwells—hammer of the monks in one century, crusader of puritanism in the next. Thomas Cromwell, the minister of Henry VIII, by his great offices acquired for himself great estates and an earldom, and left to his descendants, even after his own attainder, a barony and sufficient property (in particular the abbey of Launde, Leicestershire), to maintain it. Among those incidentally enriched by his favour was his nephew Richard Williams, who assumed in gratitude the name of Cromwell. The nunnery of Hinchingbrooke and many other lands in East Anglia and elsewhere came to Sir Richard Cromwell in consequence of his offices: he was commissioner for the dissolution of monasteries, gentleman of the Privy Chamber, general of infantry, constable of Berkeley Castle and Goderich Castle, steward of Urchenfeld, etc. His heir, Sir Henry Cromwell, inheriting the official fortune of his father and mercantile wealth from his mother (the daughter of a Lord Mayor of London), added to it by marrying the daughter of another Lord Mayor, and proceeded to live in the style to which such wealth entitled him. He built Hinchingbrooke and by his lavishness became famous as 'the golden knight'. But the style of living which could be afforded by an office-holder could not be continued indefinitely by a mere landlord; and by the turn of the century the Cromwells—both the gentry family of Hinchingbrooke and the noble family of Launde—were mere landlords. While Lord Cromwell, the heir of the great minister, was selling his last estates in England and retiring to Ireland, Sir Oliver Cromwell, the heir of 'the golden knight', was paying in land for the extravagance which could not be maintained on land. Ever-increasing loans from the London moneylenders, Sir John Spencer, Sir Richard Smyth, and Thomas Sutton, were only cleared by the sale of his estates. And who were the purchasers? Neighbouring landlords with surplus capital from estate-management? No. The Leicestershire estates of Lord Cromwell went to Lord Mountjoy, Lord Deputy of Ireland, and Sir William Smyth of London. The Essex estates of Sir Oliver Cromwell went to Sir Henry Maynard, secretary to the great Lord Burghley, Edward

[1] On the Treshams see Hist. MSS. Comm., Var. Coll. III (Tresham Papers) *passim;* their borrowings are recorded in P.R.O. Recognizances for Debt.

Ryder, Lord Mayor of London, and Theophilus, son and heir of the Earl
of Suffolk, Lord Treasurer; in Huntingdonshire, Warboys Manor went to
Sir John Leman, Lord Mayor of London, his property in Stukeley to John
Stone, sergeant at law, Waybridge Forest to Sir Henry Montagu, Earl of
Manchester, and finally Hinchingbrooke itself, after Sir Oliver had entertained his sovereign there with 'the greatest feast that had ever been given
to a king by a subject', to Sir Sidney Montagu.[1] The Montagus, indeed,
are cited by Prof. Tawney as instances of rising gentry. Certainly they
rose: within a generation there were two earldoms and a barony in the
family, and they would go yet higher: but it was not land that elevated
them. Sir Henry Montagu was recorder of London, Chief Justice of the
King's Bench, Lord Treasurer, Master of the Wards; Sir Sidney Montagu
was Master of Requests. Office and trade had enabled the Cromwells to
rise; reduced to land they had declined, and their property passed to
other families who, in their turn, had risen on the same basis: offices and
trade.

When the 'mere gentry' of England rose in rebellion against the office-
holders by whom they felt themselves excluded and exploited, a cadet of
the house of Cromwell was certainly qualified to be their leader. Their
philosopher, who dedicated his work to Oliver Cromwell, and whose views
Prof. Tawney now cites as a prefiguration of his own, was another
gentleman: James Harrington. According to Prof. Tawney, Harrington
did not merely urge the claims of the English gentry to political power, he
diagnosed that, economically, they were already there. The whole process
which Prof. Tawney postulates—the decline of the aristocracy and the
gradual acquisition of their lands by the gentry—was, according to him,
noted at the time by the perspicacious Harrington, who indeed merely
theorized on the basis of his own observation. Nor was he a distant
observer. Rejecting the theory that Harrington drew his opinions from
such remote or humble phenomena as the Irish confiscations or the
proletarian movements of his own time, Prof. Tawney remarks: 'the process from which he generalized had been taking place beneath his eyes.
His own relatives had been engaged in it.' In other words, the Harringtons themselves were a family of 'rising' gentry. The evidence given for
this conclusion is a reference to a manuscript 'which shows Sir William
Harrington and a partner buying Crown lands between Dec. 1626 and
Feb. 1627'. Now Sir William Harrington, who was not a mere gentleman
(he had no estate) but Lieut.-General of the Ordnance, may indeed have
invested in a little Crown property at the end of his life, though he does not
appear to have kept it,[2] and this small transaction may conceivably have
been known to his cousin once removed, James Harrington the philosopher;
but such a transaction is a slender basis on which to base so large a generali-

---

[1] Sir Oliver Cromwell's debts are recorded in P.R.O. Recognizances for
Debt, and Charterhouse MSS.; his sales of land in M. Noble, *Memoirs of The
Protectoral House of Cromwell* (1787), I, 37 fo.; *V.C.H. Huntingdonshire*.

[2] Holles, *Memorials*, p. 162, mentions 'Sara, the daughter (and heir *if there had
been any inheritance*) of Sir William Harrington of Bagworth'. The italics are mine.

zation, and before admitting it as evidence that the Harrington family was 'rising' on the profits of land-management in the first half of the seventeenth century, perhaps we should take a closer view of that dynasty.

The Harringtons were an ancient family established in Rutland. Under Henry VIII Sir John Harrington, the King's servant and Treasurer at War, had, thanks to these and other offices, greatly increased his property. His son, Sir James Harrington, had thus been able to buy up some further property in Leicestershire—the manor of Elmesthorpe out of the dissolving property of the 17th Earl of Oxford, and the manor of Bagworth Park from the Earl of Huntingdon—and to endow his three sons with adequate lands. His heir, Sir John Harrington, inherited the original family estates of Exton and Burley-on-the-Hill, and further, by marrying the heiress of another rich office-holder, Robert Kelway, Surveyor of the Court of Wards, added to it her great inheritance of Coombe Abbey. Sir James's second son, Sir Henry Harrington, inherited Elmesthorpe and Bagworth. His third son inherited Ridlington, one of the acquisitions of Henry VIII's minister. So far so good. In 1600 the Harringtons were clearly a 'risen' family, and Sir John Harrington of Exton could be described as 'able to dispend yearly betwixt £5000 and £7000 of good land'.[1] His fortune, it was said, equalled that of 'the best barons'; and King James, recognizing the fact, duly created him baron Harrington of Exton and made him—an expensive honour—governor to his extravagant daughter Princess Elizabeth. This was not an office of profit, it was a 'charge', such as courtiers tended not to solicit but to evade, like an embassy or a royal visit; and Lord Harrington (who was obliged to undergo both these other charges also), found them ultimately too heavy for his estate. Sir Henry Harrington of Elmesthorpe was similarly unfortunate: he followed the Earl of Essex to Ireland and incurred the royal displeasure by an unsuccessful if not positively disgraceful encounter with Tyrone's rebels. Early in the reign of James I both brothers were deeply involved with the moneylenders. Lord Harrington turned to the great London aldermen, borrowing from Sir John Spencer, Sir William Cokayne, Sir William Craven and Paul Bayning. Sir Henry Harrington borrowed successively—for no lender would give him long credit—from Sir William Glover (another great merchant), Dr Stanhope, Robert Livesay, Thomas Sutton. By 1602 he was trying—in vain—to sell his patrimony. A mercantile marriage shored up his family for a while, but not for long.[2] Within a few years he too was turning to Sir John Spencer, then to that Leviathan of Jacobean finance, Sir William Cokayne. That, as for Sir Lewis Tresham, betokened the end. After one year Cokayne claimed repayment and did not get it; then he had his debt certified into Chancery. Two years later, when Sir Henry was dead, Cokayne foreclosed on his heir and Elmesthorpe became, for three generations, the principal seat of the Cokayne family. At the same time

---

[1] Thomas Wilson, *The State of England 1600* (Camden Soc. 1936), p. 23.
[2] Sir Henry Harrington married his heir to the daughter of William Offley, citizen and merchant-tailor of London, just in time to repay Thomas Sutton out of her dowry. Sutton had already refused to buy Elmesthorpe.

Sir Henry Harrington's other seat, Bagworth Park, passed into the hands of Sir Robert Banaster, Master of the King's Household; and on the death, within the same year, of both Lord Harrington and his son and heir, now £40,000 in debt, yet vaster estates changed hands. The new favourite, George Villiers, Duke of Buckingham, moved into Burley-on-the-Hill, the great house where Lord Harrington had once entertained King James; Lady Craven, the widow of Lord Harrington's greatest creditor, set herself up in Coombe Abbey where Lord Harrington had brought up the Princess Elizabeth; and another financier, Sir Baptist Hicks, settled his family in the original family seat of Exton. Thus, within a few years, the magnificence of that family whose predominance had once been undisputed in Rutland, who in fortune had equalled the best barons and come 'not much behind many earls'; altogether disappeared, and, as the historian of Rutland sadly observed, 'all that vast estate was sold'. Only the descendants of the third brother, Sir James Harrington of Ridlington, kept the name alive. Half a century later his two grandsons commented in different ways on the crisis of their class. One, his heir, Sir James Harrington, joined the radical gentry in their rebellion, sat on the tribunal which sentenced the King, and, at the Restoration lost the last relics of the family estates. The other was James Harrington, the author of *Oceana*, who, according to Prof. Tawney—it is the ultimate paradox of his thesis—could witness in the contemporary history of his own family, 'the rise of the gentry'.[1]

Where then has this inquiry so far led us? It has suggested that whatever social changes took place in the period 1540–1640 certain formulations of them are incorrect. Aristocracy and gentry did not move in opposite directions: the distinction is anyway meaningless. Those families who 'rose' did not, as a rule, rise through the profits of land-management. Good managers there undoubtedly were, both peers and gentry, but neither their number nor their profits were sufficient by themselves to alter the social form of England by creating a new class. Indeed, it seems to me that Prof. Tawney and his disciples, by overworking the evidence and narrowing human motives, have greatly exaggerated the economic value of land in this period. Admittedly there were profits to be made in land, especially if bought or leased, as it often was, at an undervalue. Admittedly successful lawyers and business-men bought land (they generally do). But is it necessarily true that they bought it as a prudent economic investment, because 'their profession had taught them what, properly handled, land could be made to yield'? This seems to me to presuppose both the fact and the motive. Why should we suppose that every

---

[1] I have worked out the finances of the Harrington family principally from James Wright, *History of Rutland* (1684); *V.C.H. Rutland*; Nichols, *Leicestershire*, IV, 604, 987–9; P.R.O. Recognizances for Debt; Charterhouse MSS. See also *Rutland Magazine* (1907–8), III, 136–7 (transfer of Exton); *Letters of John Chamberlain* (ed. N. E. McClure 1939), II, 446; Whitelocke, *Liber Famelicus* (Camden Soc. 1858), p. 29.

purchase by a successful man is necessarily an investment for immediate profit? If that were so, surely the merchant and the lawyer would do better to lend their money, on easily revocable loans, at a guaranteed rate of 10 %, than to immobilize it in land yielding, according to current estimates, 5 % and a great deal of trouble? But even merchants and lawyers have, and had, other motives as well: they wished to acquire social consequence for themselves and to leave to their heirs an endowment which, if its yield was modest compared with that of commerce or finance or law, seemed a sure social basis for generations. Individuals might make spectacular fortunes by their wits, but dynasties—and the Elizabethan was dynastic in his outlook—clung to the safe, slow nutriment of the land. The brisk land-market of the early seventeenth century was perhaps as much the evidence of social competition as of economic speculation: it cannot be used as conclusive evidence that great fortunes were expected from land.[1]

I thus conclude that, so far, Prof. Tawney has not established his thesis. His general arguments do not seem to me conclusive, and the instances which he has given seem, on closer examination, to undermine rather than to sustain his argument. Sometimes it even seems that he has been misled by emotion, by a generous but uncritical sentimentality towards the English peasantry and a corresponding hatred of the English gentry who (he supposes) rose by their ruin: 'that blind selfish, indomitable aristocracy of county families', as he once called them, 'which made the British Empire and ruined a considerable proportion of the British nation'.[2] But in fact did the gentry rise to wealth over the crushed bodies of their peasantry? If, as my evidence has already suggested, the successful families rose rather through offices than through land, then it would seem that they gained their economic power, as they gained their political power, at the expense less of the peasantry than of the Crown. In fact, it seems to me that the whole question must be considered again, without these preconceptions, discarding altogether the false distinction between aristocracy and gentry and the hasty assumption that land was suddenly 'commercialized'. This, in the remaining portion of this article, I intend to do; and having done so, and having given my interpretation of the events of the period, I shall

---

[1] This general point—that land was generally regarded as a source of long-term stability rather than of current profit—can be illustrated from the practice of one whose whole life was spent in making money. Thomas Sutton made his fortune partly by exploiting an office in the North, partly by money-lending in London. He also bought land, and naturally improved its value where possible. A disciple of Prof. Tawney would probably conclude that he regarded land as one of his business investments. If so, I can only say that it was a poor investment for Sutton. Sutton (who was generally chary of buying land) often paid high prices for what he bought and he refused afterwards to sell it; in this therefore he was not a speculator. Further, when well over seventy years old, he was buying lands encumbered with long leases at low rents which he could not hope to outlive. Why then was he thus unprofitably investing money on which, in the ordinary course of his profession he could have made a profit of 10 % p.a.? The answer presumably is that he was thinking not of profit for himself but of security for his heirs—a charitable corporation destined to last for centuries.

[2] R. H. Tawney, *The Agrarian Problem in the Sixteenth Century* (1912), p. 316.

then consider that 'stream of contemporary comment' on those events, from which Prof. Tawney has deduced confirmation ·for his thesis, but which I believe will be found quite compatible with another.

IV

It is impossible for a mere country gentleman ever to grow rich or raise his house. He must have some other vocation with his inheritance, as to be a courtier, lawyer, merchant or some other vocation. If he hath no other vocation, let him get a ship and judiciously manage her, or buy some auditor's place, or be vice-admiral in his county. By only following the plough he may keep his word and be upright, but will never increase his fortune. Sir John Oglander wrote this with his own blood, June the 25th 1632, then aged 48 years.[1]

This *cri de cœur* of a 'mere country gentleman' is mentioned by Prof. Tawney, but only to be dismissed as exceptional and unjustifiable pessimism 'uttered at a moment when pessimism was pardonable'.[2] And yet, since it was uttered ten years before a social cataclysm in which the radical minority of the 'mere country gentlemen', less resigned than Sir John Oglander, rose and overthrew the whole order of society, this dismissal seems to me somewhat cavalier. We may not, in the interests of a questionable generalization, dismiss the Great Rebellion as an exception. In fact the economic crisis of the 'mere gentry' in the century 1540–1640, and especially in the last fifty years of it, seems to me obvious wherever we are prepared to notice it. Throughout the period their protests grew in volume; occasionally they expressed themselves in action; and the history of the period, with its gentry mutterings and gentry revolts, culminating in the greatest social explosion in our history, seems to me unintelligible unless this obvious fact is recognized.

For if 'a mere country gentleman' could not live on his land—and for every one 'good husband' who could improve his land there were others who could not—what was he to do? He might go into trade—but elder sons, the inheritors of the estates, generally shrank from that unwelcome and difficult expedient. He might marry into trade, as many of his class did. Or, best of all, he might acquire an office. I have already suggested that office rather than land was the basis of many undoubtedly 'rising' families. I would now go further. Instead of the distinction between 'old' and 'new' landlords, between peers and gentry, I would suggest as the significant distinction of Tudor and Stuart landed society, the distinction between 'court' and 'country', between the office-holders and the mere landlords. And by the words 'court' and 'office' I do not mean only the immediate members of the royal circle or the holders of political office: I use the words in the widest sense to cover all offices of profit under the

---

[1] *A Royalist's Notebook, The Commonplace Book of Sir John Oglander of Nunwell 1622-1652*, ed. Francis Bamford (1936), p. 75.

[2] *Rise of the Gentry*, p. 17. In fact the printed summaries of Sir John Oglander's accounts, running intermittently from 1622 to 1647, suggest that the year 1632 was in no way exceptional in his economy (*A Royalist's Notebook*, pp. 229–41).

crown—offices in the household, the administration, and above all—for it was most lucrative of all—the law; local office as well as central office, county lawyers as well as London lawyers, deputy-sheriffs as well as ministers, 'an auditor or a vice-admiral in his county' as well as a Teller of the Exchequer or a Warden of the Cinque Ports. These were the sheet anchors on which precarious landlords depended in a storm.

Admittedly the supply of offices was increasing. So was their value. In England, as throughout western Europe in that period, the new centralized monarchies, with their new councils and new apparatus of administration, required an ever-increasing bureaucracy; and since this bureaucracy was in part created to carry out great social and economic changes, and since the members of it were not, and could not be, strictly supervised, their opportunities, both for direct self-enrichment and for patronage, were of course enormous. What fortunes were made by the officials of Henry VIII who carried out the nationalization of monastic property! Naturally the best bargains went to them and to their local agents, the office-holding gentry in the counties. But what of the gentry who remained outside this charmed circle? They saw the opportunities which their more fortunate neighbours exploited, saw them growing rich on fees and perquisites, on grants and leases, as stewards of under-rented Crown or Church lands, as paymasters, commissioners, auditors, receivers, surveyors, feodaries; saw the gradual elevation of their style of living; and finding that they themselves not only lacked these advantages but also, as taxpayers, paid the cost of this ever-increasing apparatus, they naturally longed to exchange conditions with those happier men. But how could they do it? The first necessity was to qualify by education. Educate your children! That was the advice which the gentry pressed upon their relatives: 'make them but scholars and they are fitted for any employment'.[1] So the upper classes, who seemed hitherto to have neglected learning, now pressed into the schools previously reserved for the poor or the clergy and crowded into the Universities and the Inns of Court.[2] Even so, they might be disappointed, for just as in Spain, where the passion for offices—*empleomania*—and the glut of unemployable graduates was deplored by every economist, or in France, where the same phenomena were the despair of Richelieu,[3] so in England the demand for offices far exceeded the supply. To compete for this limited supply, the gentry attached themselves to patrons who, by their patronage or position at court, might determine its direction. Thus there grew up that system of aristocratic *clientèles* which for so long formed the pattern of English politics.

But this was not the end of the matter. There is an iron law of supply and demand, and the competition had its economic side. Offices acquired a price, and that price was increased by the competition. Offices had long been sold in France, where a regular market machinery—the *Bureau des*

---

[1] *A Royalist's Notebook*, p. 249.
[2] On this subject see Mr J. H. Hexter's admirable essay, 'The Education of the Aristocracy in the Renaissance' (*Journal of Modern History*, 1950).
[3] See his *Testament Politique*, I, ii, 10, 'Des Lettres'.

Parties Casuelles—had been developed to handle the business. In England the machinery was less developed but the result was the same. By the time of James I almost every office was bought, either from the Crown, or from the favourites who made a market of the Crown's patronage, or from the previous holder; and the price, in that era of boom and scramble, was continually rising. According to Bishop Goodman, the price of a clerkship in the Court of Wards was multiplied sixfold in his time, and 'a feodary's place, which in my remembrance was but the place of a servant, and for which was usually given not above 30 or 40 pieces, came after to be sold for £300 or £400, and, as I have been credibly informed, the last Master of the Wards took £700'.[1] In general, the price of an office, with vacant possession, appears to have been roughly equivalent to about three and a half years' purchase, and this rise in the price no doubt reflects a rise in the profits of office; but sometimes mere competition drove up the price. Thus in 1621 a member of Parliament complained that 'in the cheapness of all things offices grow dearer and are indeed of a greater price than benefices', and that because of this high capital outlay 'whosoever doth farm or buy offices binds himself to be an extortioner'.[2] The case of the Mastership of the Rolls perfectly illustrates this point. According to Sir Julius Caesar's accounts, his own profits from this office declined, between 1614 and 1631, from £2200 to £1600 p.a.; even he only claimed that they should have been £2370 p.a.; nevertheless, nine years later, when Sir Charles Caesar sought to bring the office back into the family, the price was pushed up merely by auction from £6000 to £15,000. It was, as Archbishop Laud said, 'more money than any wise man would give for it'.[3]

Those who had paid dearly for offices naturally wished to extract value from them when bought. They may not necessarily have 'bound themselves to be extortioners', but, at least, they calculated on keeping their offices for a reasonable time. Loss of office, to those who had developed official standards of living, could be a very serious blow, especially if political circumstances made it impossible for the victim to retire on terms or negotiate a sale. It was the more serious because an office-holder was not expected to save money and thus provide a cushion against retirement. The Elizabethan age was not a saving age: the ideology of saving was not generally accepted till the nineteenth century; and although merchants might have accepted different standards, it was the social duty of a gentleman not—like Lord Deincourt or Sir Francis Popham—to 'live like a hog',[4] i.e. to live below one's income, but, like Sir George Holles, to 'maintain a port to the height of what his income would permit him'. In the sixteenth century the rich man was valued not, as in the nineteenth century, by what he left at death (he generally left debts), but by what, during his lifetime, he was 'able to dispend'. Consequently, when his

---

[1] Goodman, *Court of James I* (1839), I, 271.

[2] Notestein, Relf and Simpson, *Commons Debates 1621* (1935), IV, 295, etc.

[3] E. Lodge, *Life of Sir Julius Caesar* (1827); cf. Laud, *Works* (1847–60), IV, 149.

[4] Clarendon, *History of the Rebellion* (1843), p. 301; Aubrey, *Brief Lives* (Sir John Popham).

income rose through the acquisition of an office, he at once—if he valued public opinion—increased his 'port' and expenditure accordingly. He might buy land and establish his family, but this was rather as proof of his consequence than as a financial investment: what his heir expected from him was not so much a well-husbanded estate as opportunities, through education, influence and patronage, to continue or improve upon the official career of his father—opportunities which were to be obtained not by sparing but by using his official income. This was the rule of society: to do otherwise was to cut one's self off from society and risk a dangerous ostracism. So it was complained against Sir Roger Wilbraham that, as solicitor-general in Ireland, 'he keeps no house nor spends a penny, which the country expects in all those that have Her Majesty's fees'. If Sir Roger Wilbraham died rich and left £4000 p.a. to his three daughters, it was at the expense of his reputation while living.[1]

In these circumstances uncompensated loss of office was a double disaster. First, it meant the sudden loss of an income from which little or nothing had been saved against such a misfortune; secondly, it meant either a visible retrenchment of 'port', and therefore a public exhibition of decline, humiliating in that competitive age, or (if the disgrace was to be concealed and the old habits continued) the road to insolvency. No wonder that public men dreaded, above all things, loss of office. When Lord Henry Howard meditated the ruin of Sir Walter Raleigh, the most infallible method seemed to him to be the withdrawal of his offices: Raleigh's income would then shrink from £3000 to £300 p.a., and his pride, 'above the greatest Lucifer that hath lived in our age', would inevitably drive him into desperate courses. Had not the Earl of Leicester outmanoeuvred his rival the Earl of Sussex in precisely that way, 'by stopping the springs of bounty (since he lived far above his rate)', and so causing him, in desperation, to forget himself before the Queen?[2] A generation later the loss of his office in the Court of Wards drove John Winthrop similarly to despair. 'With what comfort can I live', he asked, 'with seven or eight servants in that place and condition where for many years I have spent £300 or £400 yearly and maintained a greater charge?'[3] Such social humiliation was more than he could bear: he liquidated his estate in Suffolk and emigrated to New England.

If the sale of offices and the enhancement of their price represented the natural economic consequences of competition, this fear of losing such expensive and lucrative prizes, once they had been obtained, led to a natural human reaction: the attempt to make them hereditary. If offices rather than land were the means to wealth, the descent of an office within the family was clearly as important as the descent of an estate. Successful families therefore sought to extend the entail from their lands to their offices. In France, by the famous *Paulette* of 1604, the holders of legal office contrived to achieve this result. In Spain, by the system of 'renuncia-

---

[1] See *Diary of Roger Wilbraham* (Camden Miscellany, 1902), x, viii–x.
[2] E. Edwards, *Life of Sir Walter Raleigh* (1868), II, 443–4, 293.
[3] Quoted in J. T. Adams, *The Founding of New England* (1927), pp. 136–7.

tion', a similar result was at least made possible. In England under
James I there seem certainly to have been hopes of a Paulette: the words of
Edward Curll, Sir Robert Cecil's servant, who applied for the reversion of
his father's office as Auditor of the Court of Wards since 'by the example
of these times offices are not likely to be hereditary',[1] suggest the language
of disappointment. But even if heredity in law was unattainable, heredity
in fact was common, especially in those legal offices whose multiplication
was a chronic complaint of the time; and it seems to me that it was this
heredity of office, no less than heredity of land, that carried many a gentry
family upwards over several generations. Four members of one family in
the Court of Wards launched the families of Hare, barons Coleraine and,
ultimately, Grosvenor, Dukes of Westminster; the Tooke family were
auditors in the same court during six reigns;[2] the Ropers of Kent were
protonotaries of the King's Bench for four generations; the Molyneux
family of Sefton, one of the most successful of 'rising' gentry in Lancashire,
if they were 'good husbands' of their estates, were also Receivers of the
Duchy of Lancaster—besides numerous other offices—for at least two; the
Mastership of the Posts was for a time hereditary in the family of Stanhope;
and the Fanshawes of Ware Park whose exquisite gardens so delighted
Sir Henry Wotton and his contemporaries owed their rise and splendour
not to a Derbyshire estate worth £400 per annum but to the office of
Remembrancer of the Exchequer held continuously by five generations of
the family from the reign of Henry VIII to the time of Charles II. Once,
indeed, this essential office was nearly lost: the death of Sir Henry
Fanshawe in 1616 left his heir still a minor, and there were eager competi-
tors ready to declare him 'unfit or rather uncapable to execute it'; but
friends intervened, powerful interests were mobilized, the office was vested
in trustees until the heir should be of age, a deputy was found to perform
the duties in the interim, and thus the office was kept ultimately in the
family in spite of 'some opposition and difficulty by reason of some of the
bedchamber that were loth to lose such a morsel'. Such were the advantages of a central position at court.[3]

But what of the mere gentry who had no such positions? As each prize
became more valuable it moved further away from their reach. Education
was expensive: the mere gentry of the north and west could not always
afford to send their sons to Oxford and Cambridge; and prices in London,
that ever-growing all-absorbent metropolis, were high and rising. Offices
themselves became too costly for their purses, and reversions were often
barred to them by the dynastic solidarity of the possessing families. What
then were they to do? The most enterprising of them, of course, would not
despair: they would hope for change and attach themselves to patrons who
might profit by such change, perhaps even force such change. This was the

---

[1] Hist. MSS. Comm., Marquess of Salisbury, xv, 371.

[2] I owe this detail to Mr H. E. Bell.

[3] On Sir Henry Fanshawe, his gardens and his office, see *Memoirs of Lady
Fanshawe* (1829), pp. 9–17; Sir Henry Wotton, *Reliquiae Wottonianae* (1651),
p. 296; *The Letters of John Chamberlain* (ed. N. E. McClure, 1939), i, 557, 615.

ordinary rule of politics. If the hope was deferred, they would nevertheless continue in the running as long as they could, for change might yet be round the corner. In the meantime, still hoping, they would perhaps overspend their incomes in maintaining the struggle; perhaps they would plunge into debt and become ultimately desperate—such were the men who in the end staked all on the ventures of the Earl of Essex; perhaps they would follow Sir John Oglander's advice, to 'get a ship and judiciously manage her'—in time of war there were always the hopes of great windfalls from privateering, and it was no coincidence that the Earl of Essex's party, the party of the excluded, was also the war-party, while the party of the Cecils, the party of office, was also the party of peace; or perhaps, weary of the struggle, they would contract out of it altogether, spurn the Court and its offices, its competition and corruption, echo the words of their ultimate hero Sir Walter Raleigh

> Say to the Court it glows
> And shines like rotten wood,

and compose, in their manor houses—at least while the mood lasted—poems in praise of rural solitude and the simple life. Withdrawing from the Court, these men withdrew also from the ideology of the Court. Some of them withdrew entirely and finally, into recusancy, from which—except through reconversion—there was no way back into public life: it was in the manor houses of the disgruntled country gentry that the missionary priests of the 1580's and 1590's found their converts and their secret refuges. Others withdrew less absolutely, into an opposite ideology, the ideology of puritanism, and organized their opposition more hopefully in other country houses. But in either case the new ideology accepted by these repudiators of the court was an ideology of economy, of retrenchment. The office-holders of the Crown might live up to the limit of their inflated incomes, vying with one another in 'port' and 'housekeeping', in ostentatious building and lavish feasts; recusants and puritans alike eschewed such waste. Did not many of them date their decline from the fond attempts of their fathers to compete, on an inadequate basis, in that extravagant, and now—to these severe spirits—distasteful world?

Such, as it seems to me, was the position of many of the English gentry at the end of the sixteenth century. Of course it was not the position of the whole class, for there were unambitious men just as there were 'good husbands' among the gentry; also the position in some counties (like Warwickshire) seems to have been more stable than in others. Nevertheless, the declining 'mere gentry', for whom Sir John Oglander spoke, were sufficiently numerous to form a significant element in society, and a recognition of this fact seems to me necessary if we are to understand certain important historical problems which Prof. Tawney's method, as it seems to me, has rather obscured. First it will enable us to convert into valid terms the untenable antithesis between aristocracy and gentry; secondly, it will explain, as Prof. Tawney has never sought to explain, the rise of Independency in the Great Rebellion; thirdly it will put a different complexion on that 'stream of comment' by seventeenth-century observers which Prof. Tawney (mistakenly, as I submit) has interpreted as evidence for his thesis of the decline of the aristocracy and the 'rise of the gentry'.

For clearly if office rather than land was the source of increased prosperity among the landed classes, the rise or decline of the peerage or of the gentry will depend, at least partly, upon the access of these classes to such office. Now although I would deny any significant social distinction between peers and gentry, it seems to me that in their access to lucrative office (which is a political accident, not a social classification) it is possible sometimes to make a rough distinction between the peerage, which was small enough to form a privileged group, and the gentry, which was not. It seems to me that the peers, who, as hereditary royal councillors, were accustomed to expect great offices, and based their way of life upon that assumption,[1] were, during the reign of Elizabeth, or at least after the aristocratic revolts of 1569–72 which discredited them with the Queen, largely excluded from such office,[2] while under James I, or at least during the ascendancy of Robert Cecil, they were largely readmitted. Just as the emergence from among the gentry of a minority of mercantile and official families gives an element of truth (though with an entirely different significance) to Prof. Tawney's thesis of the 'rise of the gentry', so, as it seems to me, there is this amount of truth in the thesis that the aristocracy 'declined' under Elizabeth and 'rose' again under James I. But quite apart from the fundamental difference in our interpretations of these phenomena, it seems to me that, in their historical effects, the rise of the aristocracy under the Stuarts is far more significant than any decline they may have experienced under Elizabeth, and that the decline of the declining gentry in the early seventeenth century is at least as significant as the rise of the rising gentry. The difficulties of the excluded Elizabethan peers led to the brief inglorious rising of the Earl of Essex; the difficulties of the declining gentry not only gave substance to that abortive rising: they continued far beyond it and led directly to the Great Rebellion.

For ultimately social processes manifest themselves in political effects. The Great Rebellion is the central event of the seventeenth century in England, and any interpretation of English society which leaves unexplained that great convulsion is obviously unsatisfying. Now Prof. Tawney's thesis, in my opinion, leaves it unexplained, or rather, his

---

[1] That peers assumed court office as a right is clear, for example, from Sir Edward Walker's *Observations upon the Inconveniences which have attended the frequent promotions to Titles of Honour*, etc. (1653). Walker there argues that King James's creations of peers, by *necessitating* the creation of new offices for them, inevitably entailed loss of revenue. (Quoted in C. H. Firth, *The House of Lords in the Civil War* (1910), p. 22.)

[2] The exclusion of the nobility under Elizabeth is mentioned by Sir Robert Naunton, *Fragmenta Regalia* (s.v. Howard of Effingham and Earl of Worcester), and by the Earl of Northumberland, writing to King James in 1600. (*Correspondence of James VI of Scotland*, Camden Soc. 1860, p. 59); cf. Harrington, *Oceana* (1700), p. 69. For the Queen's parsimony of peerages after 1572 see my article 'The Elizabethan Aristocracy' in *Econ. Hist. Rev.* (1951), 2nd ser. III, 295. (To my list of peers created up to 1572 should be added the name of Lord Compton.)

explanation explains only his own thesis, not the facts. For what is his explanation? According to him, the Great Rebellion was the logical, though violent, culmination of the process which he imagines, a form of emphatic foreclosure by the creditor class of rising 'entrepreneur' gentry, City merchants and lawyers, upon the mortgaged estates of a half-bankrupt peerage, Church and Crown: 'It was discovered, not for the last time, that as a method of foreclosure war was cheaper than litigation.'

But this explanation, while consistent with his theory, seems to me quite inadequate when we come to examine more closely the actual course of the Rebellion. For apart from the fact that the English peerage, on the eve of the Rebellion, was at least as rich as at any time in the preceding century,[1] this explanation entirely leaves out of account the men who, more than any other, made the Great Rebellion—the men whose radicalism converted it from a series of political manoeuvres into civil war and social revolution: the Independents. In what sense were Oliver Cromwell and his followers in arms and politics—Henry Ireton, John Lambert, Edmund Ludlow, Edward Whalley, Oliver St John, John Bradshaw, and a hundred others without whom the Rebellion would have been impossible—representatives of a creditor class? Scarce three of the whole party, according to the indignant Clarendon, 'at the beginning of the troubles were possessed of £300 land by the year'.[2] And why, if revolution was simply the least expensive form of foreclosure, are the great creditors—lawyers and City merchants—generally found on the same side (for if not royalists

---

[1] Mr L. Stone indeed ('The Elizabethan Aristocracy, A Restatement', *Econ. Hist. Rev.* (1952), 2nd ser. IV, 311) states that, according to his own calculations, based on Prof. Tawney's method of counting manors, the English peerage, on the eve of the Civil War, was poorer than ever: it 'had more than doubled its numbers, but its landed property had failed to increase'. Now this firm statement can be tested by a more reliable method than counting manors. Mr Stone himself, in the same article (p. 304) insists that the average landed income of a late Elizabethan peer was '£2000 to £3000 p.a.'—i.e. that the total landed income of the peerage in 1600 was about £170,000 p.a. It therefore follows, if he is right, that in 1642 the total landed income of the 128 Caroline peers (if the measure of property is value) was still only about £170,000 p.a. But in fact we possess evidence of the landed income of several Caroline peers, which, thanks to the courtesy of Mr J. P. Cooper (to whom I am indebted for much other assistance in preparing this article), I am able to publish (see Appendix); and this evidence shows that 24 such peers—less than one-fifth of the Caroline peerage—had an annual income from land of at least £194,000—more than Mr Stone's argument assigns to their whole order. Even if we accept acreage, not value, as the measure of property, and so allow for appreciation, it would be difficult to squeeze the remaining 104 peers (some of them princely landlords) into the narrow margin left for them by Mr Stone.

Apart from land in England, many of the Caroline peers also had land in Ireland, e.g. the Earl of Essex, whose Irish lands (Mr Cooper tells me) were worth some £3000 p.a. in 1638; and many of them, of course, enjoyed huge incomes from offices and pensions: e.g. Lord Goring, whose landed estate was valued at only £3300 capital value, but who, in 1641, was credited with an income from offices and monopolies of £26,000 p.a. (Cal. Committee for Compounding, p. 2051; Cal. S.P. Dom. (1663–4) p. 6.)

[2] *History of the Rebellion* (1843), p. 796.

they were generally 'presbyterian') as the peers, whom, according to
Prof. Tawney, they were strangling? To imagine the Great Rebellion without the Independents seems to me an absurd speculation; but who were
the Independents? They were not 'rising' gentry; they were not a creditor
class; nor were they a sudden phenomenon of the 1640's. An examination
of their claims, which were loud, and of their previous history, which is
long, seems to me to show that the Independents, the men whose spectacular actions have given a revolutionary quality to a whole century,
represent a class which Prof. Tawney, in his interpretation of that period,
has somehow overlooked, or at least has dismissed as insignificant temporary
exceptions: the declining gentry.

This identification of the Independents with the declining gentry is not
part of conventional historical interpretation, but I believe that it is
necessary to historical understanding. I cannot, within the compass of an
essay, seek to prove it in detail; but a brief digression into political history
may at least demonstrate its plausibility.

V

The long reign of Elizabeth was in effect, and increasingly, the reign of the
Cecil dynasty. The first attempt to overthrow that dynasty was made by
a group of excluded aristocrats in 1569–72, and the failure of that attempt
only confirmed it in power. By 1590, when death had removed the rival
dynasty of the Dudleys, all patronage seemed monopolized as never before
by the Cecils and their followers. At the same time a general economic
depression accentuated the difference in fortune between the fortunate
office-holders and the unfortunate 'mere landlords' who, not belonging to
the Cecil clientele, had so long and, as they felt, so unjustly been excluded.
On the other hand, in the 1590's, the Queen and her 'Cecilian' ministers
were drawing towards their senility; great changes in the personnel of
government could hardly be long delayed; and therefore the excluded
classes looked forward more confidently to a change. In the meteoric
career of the Earl of Essex, already the most probable minister of the most
probable new king, they saw their champion, and he in them saw the
instruments of his ambition. The excluded peers, the excluded gentry,
recusant and puritan alike, gathered around him. The north country,
decayed since its vain rising a generation before, and Wales, his native
country, provided him with a field of opportunity in which family could
be mobilized against family, 'Essexians' against 'Cecilians', 'mere gentry'
against privileged office-holders.[1] Supported by these classes, and by
decayed adventurers from his own armies, Essex sought to force his way
into power. He failed, as his predecessors had failed a generation before;
and Sir Robert Cecil, by superior political skill, brought in King James to

[1] The extent to which the Essexian party, both in Wales and in the north,
consisted of 'excluded' local families emerges clearly from two excellent studies:
A. H. Dodd, 'North Wales in the Essex Revolt', *Eng. Hist. Rev.* (1944),
LIX, and R. R. Reid, 'The North Parts under the Tudors' (in *Tudor Studies*,
ed. R. W. Seton-Watson, 1924).

continue, not to break, the Cecilian monopoly. Such was the result of the first 'revolt of the squires'.

In his struggle with Essex, Robert Cecil had indeed strengthened his monopoly; but he had also learnt valuable lessons. It was politically essential to him to conciliate the peerage, in order to deprive gentry discontent of its possible leaders. This was especially necessary since, in the event of the Queen's death, his own power and that of the Privy Council would necessarily lapse, and the nobility alone would form a grand council of the realm, supreme in power until the new sovereign had declared his wishes.[1] It was also necessary to reduce the economic grievances of those 'mere gentry' without whose support the career of Essex would have been relatively insignificant. Both these policies—conciliation of the peers, relief of the gentry—were adopted by Robert Cecil. In the former he succeeded—the Essexian peers were pardoned or but lightly punished and then effectively reconciled, and when the Queen died and the Earl of Northumberland claimed power for the peers who had too long been excluded from their rights, his fellow-peers rejected his claims and referred all authority back to Cecil.[2] In the latter he failed: the decline of the mere gentry was not reversed by the accession of King James: it was aggravated.

For King James was interested in the Court, not the country. Extravagant where Elizabeth had been parsimonious, he was prepared to enrich his courtiers—at the cost of the country. He remembered that the Essexian peers had been his party, and advanced them, but he easily abandoned their inconspicuous gentry followers whom he had not directly known. Therefore, while the Essexian peers joined the Cecilian peers and the Scots peers and the new peers as office-holders in that 'lottery of unearned fortunes', the swollen Jacobean court, the gentry, who had hoped so much from his accession, and who now found themselves saddled instead with a double burden, lamented their 'betrayal'. At the new King's arrival, they had welcomed him as their saviour, for they were weary, they said, of the old Queen, 'ever hard of access and very covetous in her old days;...but after a few years, when we had experience of the Scottish government...the Queen did seem to revive; then was her memory much magnified—such ringing of bells, such public joy and sermons in commemoration of her, the picture of her tomb painted in many churches, and in effect more solemnity and joy in memory of her coronation than was for the coming of King James'.[3] To the mere gentry of England, under the Stuart 'betrayal', she was 'that unparalleled Queen Elizabeth',[4] the patron saint of what seemed, by contrast with the present, a golden age; and even under the Republic, since it was a republic of gentry, the grand regicide himself, their leader, would speak of her enthusiastically as

---

[1] This important constitutional point was fully recognized by the Council. See *The Diary of Sir Roger Wilbraham*, pp. 53–4, and cf. the Earl of Northumberland's letter on the same subject in *Correspondence of James VI of Scotland with Sir Robert Cecil* (Camden Soc. 1860), p. 73.

[2] S. R. Gardiner, History of England (1863), I, 53–4.

[3] Goodman, *Court of James I* (1839), I, 96.   [4] Holles, *Memorials*, p. 89.

'that great Queen', 'Queen Elizabeth of famous memory—we need not be ashamed to call her so'.[1]

For what were the burdens which James I redoubled on the backs of the mere gentry? The literature of the time is full of them. In particular they were two: wardships and purveyance. Now both these burdens fell with particular severity on the 'mere' gentry: the court gentry and court peers (and under James I almost all peers were court peers) were but lightly hit. For courtiers, if they paid some of the cost, also touched some of the profits of both these taxes. The great market in wardships which disgraced the Court of Wards was accessible to them, and if, as landlords, they were subject to wardships, at least, as courtiers, they were well-placed to ensure that wardships in their own families did not pass into wrong hands. They were also well-placed to beg or buy for themselves, and then to exploit, the wardship of some more defenceless family which had no such access to the court. Similarly, purveyance fell but lightly on the Court. The Court indeed was sustained by it. The officers of the household lived on it: noblemen economized at home by feeding themselves and their retinue at the royal expense—that is, through purveyance, at the expense of the country.[2] Under James I the burdens of both wardships and purveyance were doubled and quadrupled on the backs of the gentry. Purveyors, they declared, 'have rummaged and ransacked since Your Majesty's coming-in far more than under any of your royal progenitors';[3] wardships were 'the ruin almost of all men's houses once in a three descents'.[4] But their complaints were no longer heeded by the courtly peers who now profited by the system. In 1604 when the gentry in the Commons passed a bill against wardships, the Lords, in their House, obediently killed it.

But James I did not merely continue and increase and concentrate upon the gentry burdens which they had borne, though less heavily and less restively, under Elizabeth. He also added new burdens—or at least withdrew old alleviations. For what were the alleviations with which the Elizabethan gentry had sometimes sought to mend declining fortunes? Just as the Spanish *hidalgo*, if in need, saw his opportunity in one of three occupations, *iglesia o casa real o mar*—the Church, the Court or the sea—so the ambitious Elizabethan gentleman, if pressed in his estate and excluded from the court, turned to the opportunities provided by the Church, with its benefices, its under-rented lands, its stewardships, its tithes, and by the Spanish Main, with its tempting though often illusory prospects for the privateer. Unfortunately, in the first year of his reign, King James stopped both these opportunities. As Supreme Governor of the Church he appointed Richard Bancroft to the archbishopric of Canterbury; as *Rex Pacificus* he made peace with Spain.

[1] Carlyle, *Letters and Speeches of Oliver Cromwell*, Speech V.
[2] See Allegra Woodworth, *Purveyance for the Royal Household in the Reign of Queen Elizabeth* (Philadelphia, 1945), pp. 12–13.
[3] *Apology of the Commons* (1604).
[4] *Correspondence of James VI of Scotland with Sir R. Cecil* (Camden Soc. 1861), p. 59.

The work of Bancroft for the Church of England was indeed notable: rightly has it been described as 'the reconstruction of the English Church'; and a practical Anglican statesman, the first Earl of Clarendon, might well lament his premature death, after only six years in office, as 'the never enough lamented death of Dr Bancroft'.[1] The country gentry, however, viewed the matter differently. As recusants or puritans many of them had already found the Anglican Church, the Church of the Court, distasteful; under Bancroft they found it aggressive. No longer, as in the reign of Elizabeth, could they, through royal favour, detach useful morsels from vacant bishoprics: the Act of 1559, under which that had been possible, was now, in 1604, repealed, and the financial needs of the State, which Elizabeth had so often met at the expense of the Church, were now charged exclusively to the laity. Further, Bancroft began a new policy of recovering for the Church that valuable property in tithes which, at the Dissolution of the monasteries, had passed, together with the monastic lands, to the gentry.

Finally, by his peace with Spain, also in 1604, King James closed, as it seemed, the last safety-valve of the embarrassed gentry. Thereafter it was no longer possible for a mere gentleman, in default of other opportunity, to 'get a ship and judiciously manage her' as a privateer, at least under English letters of marque. King James's peace with Spain was welcome to the Court, to which it brought substantial pensions; it was welcome to the City, which prospered by the resumption of trade; it was hated by the gentry. 'Peace and law hath beggared us all', declared one of them;[2] increasingly, through joint-stock companies which were at least half privateering ventures, they sought to circumvent it; and along with the new worship of Queen Elizabeth there grew up, among them, a new cult of Sir Francis Drake and their martyr, Sir Walter Raleigh, the types of gentleman-privateer. Even their ordinary language became impregnated with metaphors drawn from that heroic age, which they regularly sought to renew. In 1632, when Sir Thomas Roe, the advocate of an 'Elizabethan', protestant foreign policy, failed to secure the vacant secretaryship of state and saw himself doomed to a private life in the country, he compared himself to Drake's ship lying idle in the dock at Deptford;[3] Sir Walter Raleigh's *History of the World* became the best-seller of the day and was the favourite reading of Oliver Cromwell; and in 1655, when foreign policy was at last determined by the gentry-republic, Oliver Cromwell referred with contempt to the peace of 1604 which he had resolved to break: 'Truly King James made a peace; but whether this nation and the interest of all Protestant Christians suffered not more by that peace than ever by Spain's hostility, I refer to your consideration.'[4] It was not 'this nation' that had suffered by the peace of 1604—which indeed had introduced a period of unexampled prosperity; it was the declining gentry.

---

[1] Clarendon, *History of the Rebellion* (1843), p. 36.
[2] *A Royalist's Notebook*, p. 14.
[3] S.P. Dom. Car. I, 173/49.
[4] Carlyle, *Letters and Speeches of Oliver Cromwell*, Speech V.

Deserted by the king from whom they had once hoped so much; deserted by their aristocratic patrons; kept from lucrative employment by the rising price and growing heredity of the offices they coveted; crushed beneath increased burdens of feudal taxation to sustain a lavish and enlarged court from which they were themselves excluded; threatened by the revival of economic claims by the Church; debarred, by the outbreak of peace, from other opportunities of investment to which they had become accustomed; no wonder if the mere gentry felt themselves betrayed under James I. Naturally they became radical in their politics. Their spokesmen began to speak violently about the aristocracy who had abandoned them. Sir Walter Raleigh, in his decline, was liable to speak of the nobility as 'fools and therefore insufficient for charge, or cowards and therefore uncapable of lieutenancy'.[1] Robert Catesby, desperately planning a purely gentry rising, said that 'he made account of the nobility as of atheists, fools and cowards, and that lusty bodies would be better for the common-wealth than they'.[2] But since they were thus deserted by their natural leaders, some at least of the gentry were prepared to act alone. Hence those spasmodic risings of the Midland gentry which followed the acces-sion of James I—the Bye Plot of 1603 and the Gunpowder Plot of 1605.

The Bye Plot and the Gunpowder Plot were both indeed recusant plots—although puritans participated in the former; for the recusant gentry were naturally the extremists of their class. While Crown and Court shed their burdens on to the protesting gentry, the politically represented gentry sought to pass on at least part of theirs, by demanding the enforce-ment of recusancy fines, on to the unrepresented recusant minority in their midst. But both were also gentry risings. The leaders of the Bye Plot—perhaps the only conspirators—were George Brooke, whose carefully laid plans to secure a rich benefice had been suddenly frustrated, and Sir Griffin Markham of Kirby Bellers, whose family, under Henry VIII, had 'ruled all the country around Newark',[3] but since then had gradually declined. Now, having lost his office and turned to recusancy, Sir Griffin Markham, who had compromised himself with Essex and was involved in debt, was vainly offering his estate to his creditors, and a writ was out for his arrest on a forfeit bond of £7000. His plot was designed not only for 'the advancement of the Catholic faith' but also 'peradventure the raising of our own house'.[4] Similarly, the Gunpowder Plotters, except for one serving-man, were all gentry: 'gentlemen of name and blood' as Guy Fawkes called them; 'gentlemen', as Cecil preferred to describe them, 'spent in their fortunes...and fit for all alterations'.[5] Many of them were old Essexians, desperate 'by reason of my Lord of Essex's death and the want of his purse to maintain them'.[6] Their leader, Robert Catesby, was

[1] E. Edwards, *Sir Walter Raleigh* (1868), ii, 44.
[2] S.P. Gunpowder Plot Book, 126. Examination of Robert Keyes, 30 November 1605.
[3] Letters and Papers of Henry VIII, xiv, 1, 295.
[4] Charterhouse MSS.; H.M.C. Marquess of Salisbury, xv, 233.
[5] *Winwood Memorials* (1725), ii, 172.
[6] H.M.C. Marquess of Salisbury, xvii, 512.

'entangled in debts'—in debt to his neighbours, to his relatives, to yeomen, to moneylenders. He had sold his valuable pastures to the Master of the Rolls and his manor of Chastleton to a clothier of Worcester. The latter he still hoped, by some lucky chance, to redeem. That chance was to be the Gunpowder Plot.[1]

Bye Plot and Gunpowder Plot were not serious threats to the government. Essex revolts without an Essex, desperate ventures by an idiot fringe, too little and too late, they were not dangers but symptoms: symptoms which the Crown failed to heed, to its cost, and which the historians of the 'rise of the gentry' have failed to heed, to their error. Robert Cecil did not fail to heed them. He unscrupulously exploited the 'Bye Plot' to ruin, at court, the possible leaders of such opposition; he unscrupulously exploited the Gunpowder Plot to break the organization of recusancy in England; but having done that he set to work to solve the problem of which these explosions were ominously symptomatic. He recognized that the grievances of the gentry were real grievances: he determined, even at the expense of his own income, to redress them. The rest of his life was devoted to that purpose. In 1604 he prorogued Parliament rather than face a battle with the Commons over purveyance, but at the same time he wrote privately to his fellow Councillors warning them that the matter was not always to be thus evaded. All pretended relief so far, he told them, was 'but shadows and colours without substance. For who does not know that purveyance is used in as many offices and by as mean instruments as ever it was? Nay, what country gentleman can you speak withal that is not able to show you continual abuses?'[2] As to wardships, in the margin of a paper denouncing the abuses of the Court of Wards and prophesying a rebellion of the gentry against it, Cecil wrote in his own hand, 'This is part of my fault'.[3] In the end, he lost the favour of the King through his heroic and disinterested but vain efforts to abolish wardships and purveyance.[4]

He had already had warning of another social consequence. If the mere gentry could find no cure for their difficulties, no relief from government, no hope in rebellion, what were they to do? They would exploit their estates, enclose the open fields, raise their rents; and if their tenants protested, they would break, by force or law, what Sir Thomas Tresham called 'their peevish and paltry proceedings'.[5] It was not that they were 'improving landlords', like the Russell family or the eighteenth-century enclosers, investing capital in their estates and so ensuring their own 'rise': they were rack-renting landlords, seeking desperately, by transferring at least some of their burdens on to the peasantry, to postpone their fall. The Midland peasantry had borne much: might they not bear just a little

---

[1] The finances of Catesby are shown by P.R.O. Recognizances for Debt and documents quoted in Margaret Dickins, *A History of Chastleton* (Banbury, 1938). Cf. H.M.C. Marquess of Salisbury, xviii, 442; *Diary of Roger Wilbraham* (Camden Miscellany, 1902), x, p. 71; Goodman, *Court of James I* (1839), i, 103.

[2] H.M.C. Marquess of Salisbury, xvi, 425.

[3] *Ibid.* xviii, 164.

[4] Cf. Goodman, *op. cit.* i, 33.

[5] H.M.C. Var. Coll. iii, 127.

more?[1] They might not. In 1607 the Midland peasants rebelled: the successive risings of the gentry were followed by the last purely peasant rebellion in England. Led by a mysterious 'Captain Pouch', calling themselves 'Levellers' and 'Diggers', they gathered at the scenes of their greatest oppression, cut down the hedges, filled up the ditches, and laid open the enclosures with which here an old landlord had tried to stay his decline, there a new landlord, finding the yield of land disappointingly low, had sought 'to raise the rent of the manor to some answerable proportion to his purchase'.[2] Among the enclosers most complained against were decaying 'mere gentry' like the Markhams of Kirby Bellers, Leicestershire, whose estate now passed to a London merchant, Erasmus de la Fountaine; the Fishers of Bishops Itchington, Warwickshire, 'ruthless depopulators' soon also to be sold up; and, above all, Sir Thomas Tresham of Rushton at whose 'town' of Newton, near Geddington, the only recorded pitched battle took place. There 'a thousand of these fellows who term themselves Levellers' were charged and scattered, with forty or fifty dead and many injured, by the Justices of the Peace and gentry. With that the revolt was over; but the defeated peasantry, like the defeated gentry, nursed their grievances. The Peasants' Revolt of 1607, like the gentry revolts of 1601–5, was symptomatic of a greater rebellion to come: a rebellion which would also have, in the rear of the radical gentry, 'Levellers' and 'Diggers', protesting once again against 'griping landlords', 'Norman enslaving lords of manors'.[3]

For in the generation between the failure of Robert Cecil's 'Great Contract' in 1610 and the mobilization of forces for the Great Rebellion in 1640 the 'mere gentry' gained no relief. There is plenty of evidence of their plight. In Northamptonshire, in 1614, Sir Edward Montagu reported on it to the Lord Lieutenant, the Earl of Exeter. In that county, he said, in which there was no special trade to alleviate dependence on agriculture, and in which many noblemen had their principal seats and great possessions, 'most of the ancientest gentlemen's houses...are either divided, diminished, or decayed'. 'There hath been within these three or four years many good lordships sold within the county, and not a gentleman of the county hath bought any, but strangers, and they no inhabitants.'[4] Eleven years later the sheriff of Nottinghamshire said the same in respect of his county. The resident gentry, he said, had been much diminished, having been bought out by 'foreigners', London merchants, like Alderman

---

[1] That enclosure was often the last resort of the declining, rather than the enterprise of the improving, landlord can be shown from numerous instances. Apart from the families mentioned in the text, the Newdigates of Arbury, Warws., are an example. The preachers of the time often drew attention to the bankruptcy which, as a sign of divine justice, overtook enclosers. In fact, in such cases enclosure had generally been a last vain expedient to forestall the bankruptcy. (I owe these observations to Mr J. P. Cooper.)

[2] L. A. Parker, 'The Agrarian Revolution at Cotesbach', in *Proceedings of the Leics. Arch. Soc.* 1948–9.

[3] G. Winstanley, *An Appeal to the House of Commons* (1649), etc.

[4] H.M.C. Duke of Buccleuch, Montagu Papers, III, 182.

Soames, and court grandees like the Earl of Devonshire.[1] 'One of the most striking things that constantly emerges from these records of the Caroline gentry', writes Dr Hoskins in his study of the Devonshire gentry under Charles I, 'is indeed their heavy indebtedness before the wars began. Most of their estates were deeply mortgaged or encumbered in some way; few were care-free in this respect.'[2] It was the same in Berkshire, where the lands were observed to be 'very skittish, and often cast their owners', and in Herefordshire, where the disproportionate fees of the under-sheriff seemed to grow 'from the decrease of the states of the gentry therein', and in Worcestershire, noted to contain 'few gentlemen of antiquity', and in Lincolnshire, where 'hardly a family maintained its position in the county, unless it had by marriage or by trade added to its income'.[3] A few official families, Monsons, Wrays, Taylors, might rise and even build, like Thomas Taylor, chancellor of the diocese, a great house; but the old families remained 'ill-housed' on their dwindling estates.

But if the gentry, in those years, gained no mitigation of their burdens, at least they gained one thing: leaders who could launch a more serious revolt. At the beginning of the reign of James I, the gentry had been powerless against the apparently solid alliance of Crown, Court and City; later in the same reign, that alliance had begun to crumble, as internal factions split the Court and the projects of alderman Cokayne dismayed the City. Thus the dissident gentry saw some of their old allies returning to lead them and to exploit their grievances. Besides, unlike the recusant gentry, the puritan gentry had an institution for the capture of power. They had Parliament, if only they knew how to use it. From 1621 to 1629 a succession of uncontrollable Parliaments warned the Court of its danger. Thereafter, for eleven years, there were no Parliaments. But it was only the voice, not the hand, of Opposition that was thus stilled. Silently, in country-houses and caucus-meetings, the new course of 'Thorough' gradually cemented together a far more formidable opposition.

For in the eleven years of personal government the burden on the gentry continued as heavy as ever. Never had the Court of Wards been so exacting: the new Master, Francis Cottington, quadrupled the old Elizabethan revenue to the Crown; and new feudal burdens were added to the old. At the same time, after a period of regression, Archbishop Laud revived the policy of Bancroft, telling the gentry that 'he hoped ere long not to leave so much as the name of a lay-fee in England'; and he stopped them from recouping at the expense of their peasantry by haling before his commissioners the enclosing landlords who 'devoured the people with a shepherd and a dog'.[4] But the years of personal government did not weigh only on the gentry. In their political folly Charles I and his clerical adviser not only exasperated the squires: they quarrelled with the

---

[1] S.P. Dom. Chas. I, x, 61.
[2] W. G. Hoskins and H. P. R. Finberg, *Devonshire Studies* (1952), p. 353.
[3] Fuller, *Worthies*, s.v. Berks, Herefordshire ('The Farewell'); T. Habington, *Survey of Worcestershire* (ed. J. Amphlett, 1893–9), I, 34; *V.C.H. Lincs.* II, 324–5.
[4] Cal. S.P. Dom. 1641–3, p. 547; 1635–6, p. 399.

City of London over its Irish lands, and by their economies at court they quarrelled with some of the office-holders and several of the peers. Thus, in the 1630's, the old aristocratic *clientèles* which the folly of Essex and the skill of Robert Cecil and the lavishness of King James seemed formerly to have dissolved, were once again, by the parsimony of King Charles, the skill of a few magnates, and the folly of Laud gradually reconstituted. As Sir Arthur Heselrige afterwards succinctly put it, 'Court Lords and country Lords differed: court lords were always biassed'.[1] As to the City, 'could Saye or Pym and their beggarly confederates', a citizen might boast, 'have found money to levy an army against their liege Lord, that had not money to pay their own debts, had not we furnished them?'[2] Thus, in 1640, with discontented peers to lead them and City money behind them, the gentry were again prepared to challenge the court, and this time the court, incompetent and divided, was unprepared for the struggle.

Of course their interests were different. The City, the peers, the disgruntled officials only wanted a return to the old alliance: the gentry, who had been the victims of that alliance were determined to destroy it. As might have been foreseen, a time came when their leaders and financiers, even the most determined of them, wished to call a halt; but the gentry were not prepared to halt. They had been deserted by their leaders before: this time they would see the matter through. At the crucial moment the timid peers heard from behind them the authentic voice of gentry radicalism: the voice of the Independents, the armed gentry, refusing to heed the aristocratic flags of truce. The New Model Army was a warning to the old court-opposition that they had mobilized forces beyond their power to control or stop.

Where were the Independents heading? They did not know. 'None climbs so high', said Cromwell, 'as he who knows not whither he is going.'[3] They had no direct understanding of politics—what a hash they made of politics when they found themselves in power! But they knew what they hated, what they wanted to destroy. Their slogans on the way to power, their fumbling actions while in power, all made it clear. Away with the Court, they cried, with its office-holders, its lawyers, its pensioners and privileged monopolists! Away with the peers—they hoped that they would 'live to see never a nobleman in England'.[4] Away with the City, the merchants who penetrated to their counties and squeezed them from their estates: 'this nation' they complained, 'was falling into the rickets, the head bigger than the body'.[5] Away with feudal dues, 'the bondage of wardships' and purveyance! Away with the Church of Bancroft and Laud which sought to recover tithes from the gentry, and with Levellers and Diggers, who sought to abolish them altogether, and away too with the

[1] Burton, *Parliamentary Diary*, IV, 82.
[2] *A Letter from Mercurius Civicus to Mercurius Rusticus* (1643), in *Somers Tracts*, IV, 580.
[3] Quoted in S. R. Gardiner, *Great Civil War*, III (1891), p. 143.
[4] Camden Miscellany (1883), VIII, p. 2.
[5] Burton, *Parliamentary Diary*, I, 343.

Presbyterian Church which merely sought to replace a centralizing Court by a centralizing City! All these things, in their radical mood, they attacked and destroyed. They executed the King, abolished the House of Lords, purged and re-purged the City, abolished wardships and purveyance, abolished the centralized Church, and preserved from Church and peasantry alike their cherished tithes. Further, as the 'country party', haters of the all-absorbent Court and City, they preached decentralization: decentralization of government (they trebled the county seats and slashed the borough seats in Parliament); decentralization of religion (what else in 'Independency'?); decentralization of trade ('I thought', protested a gentleman of Dorset, 'that long ere this we should have the trade dispersed all the nation over; and this City, it seems, must have all the trade'):[1] decentralization of law—'county registers' of land and local courts; decentralization of education: no longer must the 'mere gentry' of the north and west, by their distance from Oxford and Cambridge, be debarred from qualifying themselves for office: there must be a university in Durham, a university in Wales.[2] Finally, they must have a foreign policy. And what should that foreign policy be? What but a privateering war with Spain as in the days of 'Queen Elizabeth of famous memory', in which a gentleman could 'get a ship and judiciously manage her'? In 1655 the tradition of Drake and Raleigh was revived, and war was reopened in the West Indies. The fanatical hatreds, the impossible demands, the futile foreign policy of the Independents were the culmination of a century of protests: the protests of the declining gentry.

It was a vain dream. The gentry-republic failed. All that they gained by revolution was, in the end, another court, other office-holders, other great financiers, heavier taxes. After 1660 many of the once radical gentry drew out of radical politics. Just as the radical recusant gentry, after their vain risings in 1603–5, had relapsed into Roman Catholic quietism and become the most devoted royalists; just as the radical 'anabaptist' sects, after their vain bid for power in 1653, had relapsed into Quaker quietism; so many of the radical puritan gentry, after their failure to achieve a stable government in the interregnum—that 'settlement' after which Cromwell so desperately hankered—relapsed into gentry quietism. They became the royalist 'young squires' of the Convention and Cavalier Parliaments, the squires of the October Club, the high-flying, non-resisting tories. And in so far as they were still 'mere gentry', whom neither trade nor offices

---

[1] Burton, *Parliamentary Diary*, I, 177.

[2] The gentry of County Durham petitioned for a college at Durham in 1650 (*Commons Journals*, VI, 410; cf. Carlyle, *Letters and Speeches of Oliver Cromwell*, letter clxix). Durham College was founded in 1657. A college for Wales was advocated by a Welsh gentleman, John Lewis of Glasgrug, in two pamphlets, *Contemplations upon these Times* (1646) and εὐαγγελιόγραφα... (1656), the latter of which was dedicated to Oliver Cromwell. The project also interested Richard Baxter and others (see article by J. H. Davies in *Wales* (1896), p. 121, and T. Richards, *The Puritan Movement in Wales* (1920), p. 233). Hugh Peters, in his *Good Work for a Good Magistrate* (1651), advocates, as an ultimate ideal, colleges in Yorkshire, Cornwall and Wales.

had raised, they remained relatively poor. Macaulay, in his famous third chapter, has given of them an adequate if unsympathetic description— which, in its broad lines, has never needed revision.

VI

I have digressed thus into political history because political history is often a commentary, a corrective and clarifying commentary, on social history, and as such cannot be divorced from it. Prof. Tawney seems to me to have divorced them to such an extent that they can no longer explain each other. Ignoring the premonitory gusts—the Essex Revolt, the Bye Plot, the Gunpowder Plot—dismissing as exceptional the barometric warnings—the mutterings of gentry protest—he seems to avoid discussion even of the storm itself, the Great Rebellion, in which his thesis finds no room for the essential forces—the Independents. Instead of this commentary of political facts, Prof. Tawney appeals to a commentary of contemporary philosophy: to a 'stream of comment' by well-informed contemporary observers who, he suggests, diagnosed in their own time the same phenomenon which he has since detected: the economic replacement of a declining aristocracy by a rising gentry. It is now time to discover the significance of this comment, which seems at first sight so contrary to the evidence I have presented. To do so we must ask three questions: what is the exact sense of the comment? Who were the commentators? What were the circumstances of their commentary?

As soon as we apply the first of these tests, we find that much of the comment quoted is hardly relevant to our problem. Statements by Bacon, Raleigh and Selden that the political and military power of the nobility is greatly reduced from what it was in ancient times are not evidence of the economic replacement of the nobility by the gentry within the last century. When Selden writes that nowadays tenants will not follow their landlords to war, he does not imply that this was an inconvenience to which only noble landlords were subject; and when he writes that nowadays a tenant may be the first, 'if but a constable bid him, that shall lay the landlord by the heels', he is commenting not on the economic eclipse of the peerage by the gentry, but on the extended political authority over both of the Crown.[1] Even when Sir Walter Raleigh makes a direct comparison—'the power of the nobility being now withered and the power of the people in the flower'—the context makes it clear that he is referring to political and military, not necessarily to economic power.[2] In fact, this extension of the political power of the Crown over the great magnates, so far from spelling the economic doom of the nobility, was the prime cause of that multiplication of government offices which gave them their new opportunities. Further, as I have admitted, certain gentry families did undoubtedly rise (though apparently seldom through land-management); therefore general statements that some Members of the House of Commons

[1] Selden, *Table Talk*, s.v. 'Land'.
[2] Sir W. Raleigh, *Works* (1751), I, 207.

were of greater consequence than many peers[1] are not incompatible with
the interpretation of events which I have here advanced. They do not
prove that 'the gentry' were rising: they only illustrate the undoubted fact
that certain gentlemen were rich, certain peers poor.

Nevertheless, even when all these qualifications have been made, there
still remains evidence that some contemporary observers asserted not
merely the capture of power by the House of Commons but also a significant redistribution of land in favour of the gentry and at the expense of the
peerage. In the late 1650's James Harrington in his *Oceana*, Henry Neville
in Parliament (as afterwards in his *Plato Redivivus*), other intellectuals like
Thomas Chaloner, Republican Army officers like Captain Baynes and
Lieutenant-General Ludlow, all in turn expressed or referred to a consistent doctrine. That doctrine is, first, that in society, as a universal law
of nature, power always follows property; and secondly, that, in politics,
government—if it is to be natural, not 'perverted'—must always reside in
that social class which has the 'balance'—i.e. the preponderance—of
property. Applying these doctrines to contemporary English society, their
advocates further declared that such a shift in 'the balance' had in fact
now taken place, since the Crown and nobility had lost their property and
'the gentry have all the lands'; therefore, they concluded, the transfer of
political power to the gentry-republic was not a revolution or a usurpation
but the natural and logical and necessary recognition of a permanent fact,
and the function of politics was reducible to the discovery of a constitution
which would defend this 'natural' government against the re-imposition
of a 'perverted' system. Now at first sight these doctrines, with their
evident assumption that land is, if not the only form, at least an adequate
index of property, and their assertion that the 'balance' has shifted from
the aristocracy to the gentry, do indeed seem a prefiguration of Prof.
Tawney's thesis—provided (it is an important proviso) that they refer, as
he does, to a gradual economic process in the century before 1640, not to
a sudden political revolution after 1640. If this point can be established,
then it will be proper to regard these doctrines as relevant to our problem.

Can it be so established? On this question there must always be some
doubt, for the commentators themselves were often obscure and sometimes
self-contradictory. As long as they spoke or wrote in general terms their
words suggest a general economic process. But when exactly did this
process occur? When in fact did the Lords hold that 'balance of property'
which they had since lost? Whenever light is sought on this question, a
sudden darkness supervenes. It was 'heretofore', 'anciently', 'two hundred
years ago', 'till Henry VII', 'in the days of Popery', or of 'John of Gaunt and
such fellows': in fact, 'time out of mind', an undatable, perhaps even a
metaphysical phenomenon, like the signature of the Social Contract. And
then, sometimes, a more exact view is stated or implied: the 'old Lords'
are allowed to have held the balance not in the timeless past but on the eve
of the Civil War. 'When the Lords were in a co-ordination of power with

---

[1] E.g. the often quoted letter from Meade to Stuteville, 21 March 1627-8,
printed in T. Birch, *Court and Times of Charles I* (1848), I, 331.

you', said Captain Baynes—i.e. until the Rebellion—'they did near upon represent half the property of the nation'. It was 'in our fathers' remembrance'—i.e. in the reign of James I—according to Henry Neville, that 'near twenty Parliament men would wait upon one Lord, to know how they should demean themselves in the House of Commons'.[1] Reading all these statements it appears that the theorists are not really describing a historical process which can be ascribed to 'Tawney's century'; certainly they give no evidence of any such process, and can themselves hardly be used as evidence; they are generalizing, over a vague tract of time, a process of which their only evidence is the violent change of the last decade; and that evidence (which anyway they were accused of exaggerating),[2] being evidence of confiscation not voluntary sale, is quite irrelevant to Prof. Tawney's thesis.

Further, even if we allow the 'evidence' of these 'commentators'—who were they, and how impartial was their observation? A closer examination soon reveals that these men were not in fact independent observers: they were a group, almost a coterie of active Republican politicians, who took their views from Harrington and Neville, themselves an inseparable combine,[3] and discussed them in their private circle. From the publication of *Oceana* in 1656 to the return of Charles II in 1660, when 'all those airy models vanished', these ideas were the latest fashion among coffeehouse politicians. When Edmund Ludlow, that 'thick-skulled officer of horse', declared that the Lords were no longer, as once they had been, patrons of the Commons, 'the balance being now altered and the greatest part of the lands of England devolved upon the Commons', he was not reporting his own observation but repeating, in almost identical terms, the language of his close friend and parliamentary colleague, Henry Neville;[4] and when the same views were advanced by other officers in the Parliament of Richard Cromwell, their origin was never in doubt. 'I shall not go back to times past', declared one member who had listened to such views, 'nor look forward to *Oceana's* Platonical Commonwealth—things that are not and that never shall be.'[5] In fact, the statements made by an apparently impressive series of contemporary commentators represent not a concurrence of observation but a repetition of dogma: the dogma of *Oceana*. The question we must ask is, why was this dogma so catching at

[1] Burton, *Parliamentary Diary*, III, 335; IV, 24–5.

[2] E.g. by Arthur Annesley, *ibid.* III, 592.

[3] On the intimacy of Harrington and Neville see Aubrey, *Brief Lives* (James Harrington). That the two were joint authors of *Oceana* was presumed by Hobbes and others (*ibid.*; cf. H. F. Russell Smith, *Harrington and his Oceana* (1914), pp. 8–9). Their views are certainly indistinguishable (for Neville's views in 1658, see esp. Burton, *Parliamentary Diary*, III, 133; IV, 23–5); and when Neville, long afterwards, wrote his *Plato Redivivus* (1681) he was careful, in the Preface, to explain that his ideas had been formed before the publication of *Oceana*.

[4] Ludlow, *Memoirs* (ed. C. H. Firth, 1894), II, 59 (an almost verbal repetition of Neville's words in Burton, *Parliamentary Diary*, IV, 24–5), cf. Burton, *op. cit.* III, 283; IV, 67. For his intimacy with Neville see *Memoirs*, II, 98, 103, 173–4, 210–12.

[5] Burton, *op. cit.* III, 144.

that time? To answer this question we must examine a little more closely the characters of Harrington's disciples and the circumstances in which they embraced his doctrine.

Paradoxically, the Harringtonians—those emphatic assertors of the doctrine that 'the gentry have all the lands'—were poor illustrations of their own thesis. Like Harrington, they were, in general, lesser gentry. Henry Neville was the younger son of a family which had once indeed been among 'men of the best estates'.[1] His great-grandfather had built a great house in Berkshire; his grandfather had been ambassador in Paris; but the cost of that 'charge', the penalty of supporting Essex, and his failure to achieve office under James I had reduced the family to 'mere gentry'. Thomas Chaloner, another outspoken Harringtonian,[2] was similarly the younger son of an official family. His grandfather had become rich in the service of Protector Somerset and William Cecil; his father had improved his estate by the favour of Robert Cecil and the discovery of alum on his Yorkshire property. But in the next generation the court favour had ceased, the alum mines had been taken over by the Crown, and it was as resentful 'mere gentry' that two of the Chaloner brothers became regicides and republicans. Edmund Ludlow was the heir of a younger son, himself a radical in politics, owner only of a lease of land in Wiltshire; if he increased this property by the purchase of Dean-and-Chapter lands, it was not agriculture but revolution that had brought him these opportunities.[3] But in truth not even Harrington and Neville suggested that it was by agriculture that the gentry had so risen as to overbalance the peers in society. They did not seek to account for this alleged phenomenon: they merely stated it as a fact, or at least as a dogma.

But if the Harringtonians were, socially, lesser gentry, this is not enough to explain their politics. Within the body of the Independents they formed a smaller group. Politically, they were all Republicans: not necessarily Rumpers—the Rump, to most of them, had not been a 'Commonwealth' but an 'oligarchy'[4]—but republicans in the negative sense: radical back-benchers, a country-party within the old country party, opponents of that new court, and its new office-holders, which the problems of government were creating even in that centrifugal commonwealth, the republic of the gentry. To understand the appeal of Harringtonian doctrines, we must turn for a moment to the politics of Independency in the last year of the Protectorate.

For by 1656, the date of the publication of *Oceana*, the Independents, the radical gentry, had destroyed all their enemies. They had overthrown the court and the court-peerage which they hated; they had crushed the social

---

[1] Burton, *Parliamentary Diary*, IV, 347.

[2] *Ibid.* III, 538, 592.

[3] Ludlow bought East Knoyle and Upton (lands of the Dean and Chapter of Salisbury) for £4668. 12s. 7¾d. and was granted a lease for three lives of the parsonage of Maiden Bradley (property of the Dean and Chapter of Christ Church, Oxford). (*Memoirs*, I, 235; Muniments of Christ Church, Oxford.)

[4] Burton, *Parliamentary Diary*, III, 134; Harrington, *Oceana* (1700), p. 76.

revolutionaries who had threatened them from the left; and yet, having blundered through revolution into power, they were aware of failure. Being, by their very nature as a 'country party', unpolitical, they could not find a political system to preserve their victory. Always hankering for a civil settlement, always they found, on one side, the spectre of 'anarchy', 'blood and confusion', on the other, the bogy of its only alternative, a returned court.

What was the answer to this dilemma? A perpetual military dictatorship? Even the would-be dictator rejected that system 'so distasteful to the nation'. A revival of the Rump? Even Republicans rejected that 'fag-end of a Parliament'. The Cromwellian office-holders, disillusioned but practical men who had sometimes, as their enemies often complained, learnt politics in the service of the King, did indeed see a solution: a new, Cromwellian court seemed to them the best—indeed the only—guarantee against the return of the old Stuart court; incidentally, it would also confirm them in their still precarious offices. Thus there arose the party of Cromwell's Kingship. But to the Independent 'mere gentry' who were still 'mere gentry' one court was no better than another: it was not merely the court of Charles I, it was the court in general, which they had fought to destroy; and King Oliver was to them no better than King Charles. So, against the 'perfidious usurper' and his 'courtiers', 'the sycophants of the court', they revived and sharpened all the bitter vocabulary of the 1630's. Unfortunately, when it came to making positive proposals, they were at a loss. They had no solution. This became painfully obvious when Cromwell had refused the Crown and the battle shifted on to new ground: the proposal to set up an 'Other House', a Cromwellian House of Lords.

In a sense this proposal was even more controversial than Kingship, for whereas a *de facto* King was no novelty, and was even admitted by law, a *de facto* nobility raised thornier problems and roused sleeping passions. In particular it roused the 'presbyterians', those more prosperous, more conservative gentry who had, many of them, detested the Republic and its bloody origin, but who, in 1654, after the fear of social revolution, had accepted Cromwell as the 'saviour of society'. These men connived at the Republic, now that it was socially conservative, but they would neither condone its revolutionary past nor allow a revolutionary future. They now formed a large element in Cromwell's parliament. To them the proposal of a new House of Lords, replacing the old, seemed a further instalment of revolution. The abolition of the old House of Lords was, after all, merely a ban—which might be temporary—on the political assemblies of the peers: it did not deprive them of their peerages. But the creation of a new House implicitly deprived them of their existing status and shut the door against their return. The conservatives therefore, while prepared to postpone the return of the old Lords, protested against the creation of a new House which would exclude them for ever. The right of the old Lords, they said, was 'suspended, not extinguished'.[1]

---

[1] Burton, *Parliamentary Diary*, III, 513.

At once the Independents—Cromwellians and Republicans alike—reacted. All the old hatred of the court peers, which had fed the radicalism of the 'mere gentry' since the defeat of Essex, flared up to re-unite them. 'If you mean the old Lords', declared Colonel Sydenham, 'you had as good indeed rake in a kennel as tumble some of them up and down.'[1] Fortunately there were economic arguments which could be exploited against the old Lords. If their right to sit and legislate were admitted, then—quite apart from the increased danger of a Stuart restoration in the future—all the legislation of the last eight years, since the suspension of that right, being legislation by the House of Commons only, was by implication invalid. And that legislation included the authority for the sale of confiscated lands. Speaker after speaker reverted to the point. 'I move', declared Colonel Terril, 'to restore the old lords to their ancient right.' 'Admit this argument', replied Cromwell's Attorney-General, 'and nought has been done since '48 that is good. All public lands, sales, etc. are gone.' 'Admit Lords', declared Cromwell's adversary, Sir Anthony Ashley Cooper, succinctly, 'and admit all.'[2]

But if Cromwellians and Republicans agreed in their hatred of the old court-peers, and the fears of their economic consequences, their positive reactions were different. To the Cromwellians the Presbyterian intervention had its uses. The threat of the return of the old Lords served to emphasize the necessity of the new, and the shrill cries of the Republicans, being unaccompanied by any practical proposal, only advertised the solution of their rivals. What then were the Republicans to do, those unpractical men who hated alike new courts and old, and saw the spectres of both looming ever larger on either side? They needed an argument which could not be exploited against them by the Cromwellians, an argument equally destructive of the claims of the old House of Lords and of the new 'Other House', an argument, furthermore, which did not entail the return of that exploded oligarchy, the Rump.

This argument James Harrington and Henry Neville providentially supplied. Their doctrine of the 'balance' came as a formula of salvation to the 'mere gentry', the Republicans trembling between the old court and the new. For according to this doctrine the old peers had not been legally deprived of their rights—in which case they could legally recover them: they had, by an irreversible natural process, lost them. The Republic, by the same process, had become sovereign, and the land-sales and other laws which it had proclaimed were the authentic utterances of a sovereign power. The new peerage, by the same natural rule, being a peerage 'which has not the interest of two Knights', a peerage 'that must borrow 12*d.* to buy a blue riband to distinguish their honour',[3] had no right to exist: it would be, in the technical language of Harrington's philosophy, an 'oligarchy'.[4] Thus Harrington's doctrine, the utopian doctrine of a perpetual 'country party' of 'mere gentry' governing—in order to prevent

---

[1] *Ibid.* IV, 299.
[2] *Ibid.* III, 525; II, 419.
[3] *Ibid.* III, 31; IV, 36.
[4] J. Harrington, *Oceana and Other Works*, ed. Toland (1700), pp. 40, 498.

the emergence of a court or an official class—by rotation of offices, became, for a time, the slogan not only of the 'mere gentry' protesting equally against the old court and the new court, but the slogan also of the now dethroned 'oligarchs' of the Rump, whom Harrington detested, and who wished to reconstitute a third, a republican but by no means rotating court, and the slogan of a few great land-speculators, who by trafficking in debentures had built up great properties and now feared their loss. Such was Captain Adam Baynes, Army-contractor, commissioner of Customs and Excise, who, by handling the debentures of Lambert's Northern Army, had acquired for himself a series of royal forests and domains and 'delinquents' lands', and became—for a time—a landed magnate in the north. He did not want a rotatory government of mere gentry: he wanted government by men of property, who would guarantee the redistribution of which he was a beneficiary; but he found Harringtonian doctrines the best basis òn which to argue such a case. 'If you can find a House of Lords to balance property, do it. Else let a senate be chosen by the election of the people on the same account. There must be a balance.' There is nothing here of the 'rise of the gentry'. Baynes was a practical man, and his sole concern was that the House of Lords, however constituted, should be rich, and should ask no questions. Then the world would be safe for Adam Baynes.

Thus the doctrines of their champion, James Harrington, became, for a brief time, the slogan of the 'mere gentry' in their last losing struggle against the Court. The fact that they lost in that struggle is evidence of the falsity of the doctrine: for if power always follows property, and the gentry had all the property, the gentry should clearly have prevailed against the successive 'oligarchical' courts by which in fact they were ruled. But in fact power does not necessarily follow property: property—as the economic rise of the office-holder shows—often follows power; and 'the gentry' had not acquired 'all the lands' (which anyway is not synonymous with the balance of property)—although it is true that some gentry, through mercantile or official activities, had increased their share of them. The statement that 'the gentry have all the lands' was in truth not an objective observation of fact, but—like the statements that 'the saints shall rule the earth', or 'all power is from the people'—a political dogma whereby a class seeking power sought to sanctify its claims. When Hitler stated, in 1940, that England was defeated, and, in 1941, that Russia was finished, these statements were not true statements of fact; they were slogans uttered, regardless of truth, to inspire waverers in a difficult and uncertain struggle. The cry of the relatively poor mere gentry (which was curiously not echoed by the rich official gentry) that 'the gentry have all the lands' was similar. I hope that the evidence which I have given in this article is enough to prevent it being any longer accepted as informed comment on a general 'rise of the gentry' at the expense of the peerage. In the sixteenth and seventeenth centuries at least such a *general* rise of mere gentry has not yet been proved, and the political history of the period is a better commentary on such matters than the desperate slogans of a doomed party in its last convulsions.

VII

Thus, if my analysis is correct, Prof. Tawney's thesis must be revised: the gentry did not rise as a class, nor at the expense of the aristocracy, nor on the profits of agriculture. It now remains to summarize the positive conclusions to which my examination leads us. This can be done very briefly.

In the sixteenth century one general phenomenon at least can be isolated. The Price Revolution, which trebled prices in a hundred years, naturally struck all those landlords, whether peers or gentry, whom law or custom or habit of mind debarred from raising their old rents to the new economic level, but whom (unlike the yeomen) taste or convention or ambition still obliged to spend their money freely. What were such landlords to do? One answer was to improve their lands: to cut down expenditure, take in hand their demesne, enclose waste and commons, grow timber and wool, introduce more exact methods both of farming and accounting, raise rents and fines, redistribute the cost of administration, take up money, when necessary, in the growing London money-market.[1] Thus gradually they would rise again above the economic waves. Many landlords of course did this. From about 1580 the rents of land show a marked rise which continues till the end of the price revolution in the middle of the seventeenth century. From about 1600 new methods of agriculture are recommended in those manuals of husbandry which hitherto, for three centuries, had hardly varied. This is that 'good husbandry' of which so much has been written and upon which so vast a theoretical superstructure has been precariously based. But what was the result of this achievement? The improving gentry survived. By the early seventeenth century, when the rise in prices was apparently slowing down and the profits of improved land were catching it up, their crisis was over. Instead of sinking, and thereby becoming desperate, like the unenterprising country gentry, they had weathered the storm and were once again as prosperous as before. Sometimes they were perhaps even more prosperous. But did they do more? Did they become, on this basis, a new social *élite*? I doubt it. If they had escaped being the victims of the secular change, equally they were not its signal profiteers. They were the solid substance of rural society, its soundest members, and, because sound, generally unobtrusive in national affairs. The greater gentry, the rising gentry, who directed

---

[1] I am quite prepared to repeat here my earlier statement that borrowing '*if kept within limits*' was economically advantageous to landlords who might otherwise be forced to sell at great disadvantage. This was explicitly admitted, in his own case, by Sir Christopher Wandesford, who ascribed his improvement of his estate, in part, to his good credit with moneylenders, whereby 'I supplied my occasions with money at the usual rates, which I was forced to do continually, rather than by sale of some part of my lands, by mortgages, or some more disadvantageous bargains, to weaken my estate and lessen my revenues'. (*Instructions to his Son* (ed. 1777), p. 159.) And cf. Bacon, *Essays*, 'Of Usury': 'were it not upon this easy borrowing upon interest, men's necessities would draw upon them a most sudden undoing, in that they would be forced to sell their means (be it lands or goods) far under foot.'

political history, and the lesser gentry, the declining gentry, who gave it its revolutionary substance, were different classes from these.

First the greater, the rising gentry. These, as I think I have shown, were a small minority, an oligarchy of prosperous families, whose wealth raised them well above the common run of their neighbours. On the eve of the Civil War the average income of the gentry of Devonshire appears to have been about £150 p.a.—nearer London, 'where their lands are set to the highest', it was no doubt higher;[1] but the great gentry were 'able to dispend' with comfort £2000 or £3000 a year.[2] This wealth came only in part from land: in general it came, directly or indirectly, from offices or trade—those offices and that trade which, in the preceding century, had been continually centralized in the ever-growing capital. 'Tudor despotism', A. F. Pollard once wrote, 'consisted largely in London's dominance over the rest of England';[3] and this London was not only the City of London which seemed to contemporaries to be absorbing all the trade of the kingdom: it was also the City of Westminster which, growing just as fast, seemed equally to be absorbing all the offices and becoming the general market of them. Trade, law, politics, all were centralized in that double metropolis; there the greater gentry made their lucrative acquaintance with all three of them; there they found their City marriages, their official fortunes, their political alliances; and if they were also 'country-gentlemen', with houses and estates in the country, that accounted for part of their lives only: for an important part—politically and economically the most important part—they were 'court-gentlemen'.

Quite different was the position of the real country gentlemen, the 'mere gentry', who had no other source of income but the rent of their land, 'les pauvres gentilhommes', as the sympathetic Cardinal Richelieu called them (for they were a major problem in France also, in spite of the much-puffed 'Renaissance agricole'), 'dont le bien ne consiste qu'en fonds de terre', and who 'ne peuvent s'élever aux charges et dignités qu'au prix de leur ruine'.[4] Hit by the price revolution, slow to redeem their losses by 'good husbandry', left in the provinces from which, they complained, the hated metropolis had drained the wealth and vitality, taxed to maintain 'the expenses of a court so vast and unlimited by the old good rules of economy',[5] the English mere gentry felt themselves to be a depressed, declining class, and, grumbling, consoled—or armed—themselves with

---

[1] 'The Estates of the Caroline Gentry' in W. G. Hoskins and H. P. R. Finberg, *Devonshire Studies* (1952); Thomas Wilson, 'The State of England' (Camden Miscellany, 1936), p. 22.

[2] In 1600 Henry Beaumont of Cole-orton, with over £1500 p.a. 'had rather be a rich gentleman than a poor baron' (Hist. MSS. Comm. Marquess of Salisbury, x, 391). Between 1635 and 1641 Sir Thomas Barrington's recorded annual expenditure varied from £1146. 1s. 6d. to £3379. 7s. 11d. (F. W. Galpin, 'Household Expenses of Sir Thomas Barrington' in *Essex Arch. Soc.* N.S. xII, 202–24). Numerous other instances could be given.

[3] A. F. Pollard, 'Local History', in *Times Literary Supplement*, 11 March 1920.

[4] Richelieu, *Testament Politique*, III, 1, 'De la noblesse.'

[5] Clarendon, *History of The Rebellion* (1843), p. 5.

religious dissent. Against a protestant court some of them struck under the banner of recusancy; against a 'popish' court others struck again, under the banner of puritanism. The first attack had failed, for it had had no fit leaders, and court and society had firmly resisted it; the second succeeded —for a time. In 1640, after the experiment of Charles I's personal rule, the court gentry, like the court peerage, was hopelessly split; rival court factions armed the mutinous country gentry—and indeed the mutinous artisans—and then, failing to control the resentful spirit they had thus conjured up, were themselves overthrown by it. But the revolution did not last. Unpolitical, unconstructive, retrograde, the Independents had no policy except an impossible decentralization; and when the old court parties, the royalists and the 'presbyterians', had drawn together again, their brief interval of misused power was over. When Cromwell's throne was vacant and his army neutralized, his 'courtiers' transferred their allegiance; by the agreement of old and new courtiers, a new court, the court of Charles II, was effortlessly established; and the provincial gentry retired again to their provinces and their poverty. They—the mere gentry—had not 'risen' at all; and if, in the nineteenth century, the solid conservative structure of English rural society seemed to foreigners so eccentric and remarkable, that solidity (I suspect) was due to developments after, not before, the Great Rebellion. The Tory squires of Victorian England were indeed prosperous and educated men, and when they read Macaulay's famous but merciless description of their ancestors, the clownish tory squireens of 1680, they were as outraged as contemporary parsons when they were assured by Darwin that their ancestors had been apes. They protested, loudly and desperately, that Macaulay was wrong, actuated by mere Whig spite. But is it not equally possible that squires had changed since 1680—indeed that the great change in their status had occurred since then? Remembering the mutinous squires of the reign of Queen Anne, Addison's foxhunters[1] and Fielding's Squire Western, I am ready to end this essay by hazarding a hypothesis: that while the sixteenth century, with its offices for the few, may have elevated an *élite* of official county families—an elastic, changing *élite*, like the English peerage, but still an *élite*—it was the eighteenth century, whose agricultural revolution and tax-relief brought benefits to every landlord, that witnessed that more general phenomenon, the Rise of the Gentry.

[1] 'For the honour of His Majesty and the safety of his government, we cannot but observe that those who have appeared the greatest enemies to both are of that rank of men who are commonly distinguished by the title of foxhunters' (Addison, *The Freeholder* (1716), no. 22).

APPENDIX

The landed wealth of the English Peerage under Charles I

The following list, compiled by Mr J. P. Cooper, shows the annual income from land enjoyed by twenty-three English peers in the reign of Charles I. The peers have not been selected for their wealth or indeed on any other account: they are simply those in respect of whom such information happens to have come to hand, and they happen to include great and small estates, old and new titles. It is possible that some figures may be exaggerated—e.g. nos. (1) and (3), where the parties had an interest in assessing their estates at the highest figure; but eleven of the instances, representing over one-quarter of the value, come from particulars for compounding, and are more likely to be under-estimates. Where known widows' jointures have been included in the estate.

	Date	Income from land alone (£ p.a.)	Source of information
1. Earl of Worcester	1642	23,000	H. Dircks, *Life of the Marquis of Worcester* (1865), p. 54
2. Earl of Newcastle	1642	22,393	Margaret, Duchess of Newcastle, *Life of the Duke of Newcastle* (ed. Firth, 1907), pp. 75–7
3. The Talbot estate*	—	20,000	Strafford MSS., vol. 20, Sheffield Central Library
4. Earl of Devonshire†	1626	16,600	Accounts of the 1st Earl of Devonshire and Hobbes Papers, D.6., Chatsworth
5. Lord Petre	1638	13,000	W. R. Emerson, 'The Petre Estates', D.Phil. Thesis (Oxford 1951)
6. Lord Craven‡	1652	over 11,000	Contracts of Treason Trustees, Longleat Misc. Books, vol. 6
7. Earl of Thanet	1644	10,000	*Calendar, Committee for Compounding*, p. 839; P.R.O., S.P. 23/2/5
8. Earl of Bedford	1641	8,500	G. Scott Thomson, *Life in a Noble Household* (1937), p. 45
9. Lord Berkeley	*c.* 1635	8,000	Smith of Nibley MSS., Gloucester Public Library
10. Earl of Clare	1637	8,000	G. Holles, *Memorials of the Holles Family* (Camden Soc. 1937), p. 95
11. Earl of Northampton	1631	6,330	Marquess of Northampton, *History of the Comptons* (1930), pp. 79–80
12. Earl of Derby	1640	6,000 (at least)	*Royalist Composition Papers*, vol. 2. Lancs. and Cheshire Record Soc.
13. Viscount Wentworth	1629	6,000	W. Knowler, *Strafford Letters* (1739), II, 106; confirmed by Strafford MSS. vol. 29, Sheffield Central Library
14. Earl of Westmoreland	1644	6,000	'or thereabouts...in possession and reversion' (S.P. 23/2/5)
15. Marquess of Hertford§ and Francis Lord Seymour of Trowbridge	1642	5,400	P.R.O., S.P. 23/191/615, 785, 797
16. Viscount Bayning (title extinct 1638)	1637	5,000	Vere-Bayning MSS., Essex Record Office

17. Earl of Lindsey	1637	3,900	P.R.O., S.P. 23/193/187
18. Earl of Chesterfield	1649	3,700	*Calendar, Committee for Compounding,* p. 1274
19. Earl of Dorset	1642	3,400	P.R.O., S.P. 23/193/248
20. Lord Chandos	1642	2,800	E. Dent, *Annals of Winchcombe and Sudeley* (1877) p. 280
21. Viscount Fauconberg	1642	2,800	*Royalist Composition Papers* (Yorks Arch. Soc., Record Series), ii, 167
22. Viscount Savile	1642	1,600	*Ibid.* ii, 9
23. Lord Mohun	1646	1,000	*Calendar, Committee for Compounding,* p. 1504
	Total	£194,423	

* This figure comes from a statement, made by Edward, 8th Earl of Shrewsbury, in 1617, concerning the settlements made by his brother, Gilbert, the 7th Earl. The bulk of the property mentioned went to Gilbert's three daughters and co-heiresses, the Countesses of Pembroke, Kent and Arundel, and ultimately devolved through Alethea, Countess of Arundel, upon the Howard family, Dukes of Norfolk. Some part, however, appears to have remained with the Earldom of Shrewsbury. The estate of the co-heiresses c. 1642 was £17,000 p.a. *plus* £5000 p.a. for leases of woods for ironworks. (Bodleian, MSS. Selden supra 115; Wentworth Woodhouse MSS., Bright MSS. 24–30; P.R.O. S.P. 23/62/627 ff.)

† Land valued at under £2000 p.a. was sold to pay the 2nd Earl's debts, in virtue of power given by Act of Parliament of 1628. But the second Earl's widow purchased lands of equal or greater value in the 1630's which ought to have been settled on the 3rd Earl.

‡ This figure consists solely of certain annual rents; it excludes all improvable values and casual revenues. It has not been possible to ascertain whether the contracts of sale in this volume include all Lord Craven's estates.

§ The particulars of Francis, Lord Seymour, and of his son and heir apparent, Charles (£1200 and £1500 p.a. respectively) have been included in these figures, because only some £800 seems to have been held by them in fee: the rest consisted of leases for lives and life-interests with reversions to the Marquess and his heirs. The Marquess's particular of £3650 p.a. does not include the unknown amount settled on his son and heir apparent Lord Beauchamp. The particular does not give the real annual income of the estate, since much of it was let for lives, while the particular mainly consists of old rents. The assessment of the fine (*Calendar, Committee for Compounding,* p. 1330) suggests an income of possibly double the particular.

For material in this note acknowledgements are due to the owners of the Longleat MSS. (The Marquess of Bath), the Wentworth Woodhouse MSS. (Earl Fitzwilliam and the Trustees of the Fitzwilliam Settled Estates) and the Chatsworth MSS. (The Trustees of the Chatsworth Settlement).